The Art of
Keeping Snakes

By Philippe de Vosjoli

COMPANIONHOUSE
BOOKS

THE ART OF KEEPING SNAKES

CompanionHouse Books™ is an imprint of Fox Chapel Publishing.

The author wishes to thank the many friends who came to the rescue and provided animals and/or photos for this project. Special thanks go to Bill Love and David Northcott for their outstanding photos and to Kristin Mehus-Roe for the careful final editing that made this book possible.

The author would also like to thank his good friends Susan Donoghue, V.M.D. for editorial guidance and general brainstorming, and Roger Klingenberg D.V.M for his support through the author's many writing and herp ventures.

Project Team
Editorial Director: Kerry Bogert
Editor: Kristin Mehus-Roe
Special Consultant: Nick Clemente
Design: Michael Vincent Capozzi
Index: Rachel Rice

Cover photography by David Northcott
Bill Love, pp. 9, 12, 112 both; 119, 121, 125, 126, 127, 128, 130, 131 both, 132 both, 156 both, 167, 168, 172 bottom, 175, 177, 182, 186, 191, 198, 200 both, 203, 205 bottom, 206, 210, 211, 214, 215; David Northcott, pp. 148, 149, 150, 153, 155, 158, 159, 163, 164, 165, 166, 170, 172 top, 179, 183 both, 187, 192, 193, 195, 196, 204, 205 top, 209, 213. All other photos by Philippe de Vosjoli.

ISBN 978-1-62008-204-1

The Cataloging-in-Publication Data is on file with the Library of Congress.

This book has been published with the intent to provide accurate and authoritative information in regard to the subject matter within. While every precaution has been taken in the preparation of this book, the author and publisher expressly disclaim any responsibility for any errors, omissions, or adverse effects arising from the use or application of the information contained herein. The techniques and suggestions are used at the reader's discretion and are not to be considered a substitute for veterinary care. If you suspect a medical problem, consult your veterinarian.

Fox Chapel Publishing
903 Square Street
Mount Joy, PA 17552

www.facebook.com/companionhousebooks

We are always looking for talented authors. To submit an idea, please send a brief inquiry to acquisitions@foxchapelpublishing.com.

Printed and bound in the United States
24 23 22 21   2 4 6 8 10 9 7 5 3

CONTENTS

Part I: *A New Way to Keep Snakes*

Part II: *The Best Display Snakes*

Part I:

A New Way to Keep Snakes

CHAPTER 1:

WHAT IS THE ART OF KEEPING SNAKES?

During the last twenty-five years, the popularity of keeping snakes has surged in North America, Europe, and, more recently, Asia. More than fifty kinds of snakes are now regularly bred in captivity and over one hundred species are now regularly available through pet stores, specialized dealers, private hobbyists, and the many herp shows and events that have sprung up in recent years.

For those of us who have worked with snakes since the 1960s, the sudden rise in popularity was not shocking. It was only a matter of time before the secret got out: snakes are among the most beautiful and fascinating of all the vertebrates. Once people overcome their bias and superstitions, they quickly recognize the aesthetics of snake pattern, color, scalation, grace of movement, and behavior.

Originally, as with other animal-related hobbies, the herpetoculture of snakes had to overcome a major hurdle: determining the basic methods for keeping snakes alive for extended periods of time and successfully propagating them over several generations. Indeed, no animal-based hobby can survive or progress to the next level until this primary issue is overcome. It is only in recent years, after firmly establishing a wide variety of snake species in captivity, that American reptile keepers have followed in the footsteps of European hobbyists and begun to create naturalistic vivaria for displaying snakes.

The purpose of this book is to introduce the reader to the cutting edge of naturalistic vivaria methods. It is the combination of the intrinsic beauty of snakes and the art of designing eye-catching naturalistic displays that hobbyists call the "art of keeping snakes."

I am often asked why I keep snakes. My answer is, "Because they never fail to fascinate me." Snakes have grabbed our attention since the dawn of humankind and will not be ignored. We watch snakes with wariness—attracted and terrified at the same time. Our evolution, both biological and cultural, has been shaped in subtle ways by snakes. In several tropical areas, including Africa—the continent of our origin—deadly venomous snakes are the equivalent of living land mines. You watch for them, you carefully avoid them, and sometimes, if you step in the wrong place, you die from them.

Snakes have a psychological impact on us. They are legless aliens: suspended, fast disappearing, lurking, slithering, climbing, striking, constricting, and venomous instant death. They are the beasts that swallow their prey whole and crawl out of their skin renewed. Their image was carved into bones carried by our prehistoric ancestors and painted on cave walls. Snakes are among the most common and enduring of all mythological themes, their imprint so ancient that they rule our folklore. From Australian dream snakes to the infamous biblical tempter and the Quetzalcoatl (plumed serpent) of the Aztecs to the Great Anaconda of Amazonian Indians, they are emotional catalysts. They serve as the confrontation between states of fear and attraction, life and death, ignorance and knowledge, and nature and culture.

There are many reasons why people keep snakes, but it is worth noting that snake keepers are overwhelmingly male, which makes for some interesting psychological interpretations. Although people sometimes joke about men showing off their large pythons or boas in public, I suspect that many male keepers are attracted to the snake's remarkable hunting prowess. Anyone who has witnessed a viper or a constrictor strike a mouse or rat with blinding speed or consume its prey headfirst is amazed at the efficiency and expediency with which snakes kill and consume. It suggests miraculous powers, an incarnation of death itself, making bodies disappear and removing all evidence of existence. There is little doubt that, for men, part of the appeal of snakes is that they are lean, mean killing machines. If snakes were demure vegetarians feeding on tofu, they would not appeal to some of the more aggressive instincts of men.

Keeping snakes has other rewards. When contained in an enclosure, we are allowed to observe them and witness their beauty. As many snake aficionados and impassioned herpetologists will tell you, upon close inspection snakes are among the most beautiful of all the vertebrates on earth. But it is only under the special conditions of captivity that we are able to observe this beauty. In the wild, snakes are notoriously wary; glimpses of snakes tend to be fleeting unless captured by expensive camera equipment. One of the great secrets of snakedom is that the closer you look, the more beautiful snakes are. Close up, the linear creatures reveal their intricacies of pattern and color. Not only is there beauty of form, color, and pattern, but these features

Rhyncophis boulengeri, a rare semiarboreal colubrid from Vietnam, it is well suited for keeping in a naturalistic vivarium.

are part of an intricate geometrical overlay of finely textured scalation. The details of individual scales—their structure, keels, sheen, jewel-like iridescence, and velvety flatness—integrated with myriad patterns of color generate a kind of cellular art.

The head is the most intricate area of the snake's body. Viewed up close, it is a rich and deeply carved topography designed around the most beautiful eyes in nature— vertical black pupils encircled by gold, black, silvery white, yellow, and even pale blue.

Snakes are also mobile art. They display grace, economy of movement, and precise muscular coordination. They don't walk, run, or hop. Instead, they are moving lines—an S that zips, zigzags, and glides through the landscape.

With anticipation, curious attraction, and fascination, the snake keeper enters the scene, breaking down ancient boundaries and attempting the inconceivable. Instead of being feared and slaughtered, the legless dragon is invited to live as a guest in the keeper's home. The host cannot help but feel a kind of awe.

Art and the Animal

How does the keeping of an animal become art? It's really not that hard to imagine. After all, the Japanese make an art out of serving tea, assembling rocks in patterned sand, and training trees in small containers. To me, art is the actualization of a personal vision or message. It doesn't matter whether it's poetry, writing, drawing, the design of a car, or the way a person dresses. Art takes something out of the ordinary and forces you to notice it. A cube is a cube, but in the right context it can become abstract art.

The art in keeping snakes is the way in which it alters the normal context of snakes. It takes them out of nature and puts them in our culture, in a home or a zoological display. In nature, snakes are avoided or observed at a distance, but in containers behind the security of half-inch glass they draw crowds wherever they are displayed. The feared serpent captured and securely contained can now be safely examined up close. In this context, the snake is art. It draws attention and elicits powerful feelings and interpretations. People can put aside their fear and consider snakes for what they really are.

The idea for keeping snakes as art came to me as a result of my ongoing work developing naturalistic vivarium systems with lizards and amphibians, and through my study of snakes. At the beginning, I asked myself, "If other reptiles and amphibians can be kept in attractive displays that often develop systemlike qualities, is it possible with snakes?" My initial experiments with boas, pythons, and radiated rat snakes showed that it was feasible. It also radically changed my approach to keeping snakes and other herps (reptiles and amphibians) and raised important ethical issues. The turning point in my thinking was associated with radiated rat snakes. I had seen these snakes maintained like countless other herps under the widespread Laboratory Animal Method (LAM), an approach that I also call TEKLO (yes, it intentionally sounds like low tech), the TEchnology of Keeping herps as Living Objects.

The LAM approach essentially treats snakes as if they were small animals, such as mice or hamsters. Accordingly, they are kept in the same manner as these creatures are typically maintained in laboratories. The snakes are placed in relatively small enclosures with absorbent wood shaving-type substrate, a shelter box, and a water dish. With the TEKLO method, snakes (and other herps) are treated as objects because the sentient aspects of the living animal are largely ignored, as they are with the keeping of confined laboratory and production farm animals.

Consider radiated rat snakes: this curious, highly visual species spends great periods of time watching its environment. My radiated snakes, which are kept in a naturalistic vivarium, stick their heads out of their shelters and watch as I perform maintenance chores. They bask on branches and stacked rocks when the midday sun comes through a window and strikes the upper portion of their enclosure. They also watch from perching sites. In their vivarium, they exhibit established behavior patterns and show signs of a certain adaptive intelligence. Indeed, a number of

Typical laboratory animal setups use wood bedding such as aspen shavings as substrate. Usually a shelter and a water dish are the only design/landscape structures included. These types of setups are ideal for breeders who need to maintain large numbers of snakes in small areas.

snake species have shown an increased range of behaviors and intelligence when they are kept in larger naturalistic vivaria. Among them are common kingsnakes, corn snakes, diadem snakes, and a number of boid (boas and pythons) snakes. Seeing how snakes behave in larger, more complex vivaria—called "enriched environments" by zoos—raises the question of ethics in the popularizing and widespread marketing of the LAM method by the pet trade. The LAM method has transformed snakes into a variation of confined hamsters and mice, a disturbing thought for anyone who has a sense of the nature of snakes. The LAM method may be useful when housing large numbers of animals, such as in scientific research, reptile import, retail businesses, and commercial breeding operations. However, it is not the right way to keep and display snakes if you care about their welfare and quality of life, and it will limit your enjoyment in observing these fascinating creatures.

Adaptation

With few exceptions, larger vertebrate animals must adapt to survive. The potential adaptive limits of an animal, which I call their adaptive range, are a result of adaptive plasticity. As an example, human beings are able to survive due to our remarkable adaptive plasticity. We manage to survive under desert and arctic conditions, in sterile prisons, and in the luxurious lifestyles of the wealthy.

Snakes taken from the wild or born in captivity must be transposed into a set of conditions that are within the limits of their adaptive range. Overly cold, hot, wet, or crowded conditions can lead to the eventual death of a snake.

Part of the adaptive range of a species is its adaptive intelligence. Take a snake and put it in a captive environment, what does it do? Although it may initially hide, it will eventually explore the opportunities offered by the environment and adapt its behaviors to it. Put a snake in the prisonlike sterility of LAM conditions and the snake, just as human prisoners, adapts its behaviors to the reduced opportunities presented. Place a snake in a more complex environment and the less-specialized species, including most of the snakes available in the pet trade, will usually adapt and expand their behaviors to the greater range of conditions.

The Art of Keeping Snakes focuses on the naturalistic approach to vivarium design. This approach includes elements that simulate certain aspects of nature and convey a natural aesthetic sense. The design media include soil-like substrates, wood, rock, and live plants assembled to structure the topography of the vivarium. The art of keeping snakes tests the adaptive limits of each species and shapes its behavior so that it is easier to observe. If snakes are provided with only overhead basking lights, many species will adapt to the heat source and develop basking patterns related to that source, making them visible during the day. Many rat snakes, common kingsnakes, rosy boas, and boa constrictors will adapt their behaviors to the heat source. For other species, this adaptation is outside of their range; their resistance to exposing themselves to light is greater than their drive to be warm.

Just as snakes will adapt to a set of vivarium conditions, the vivarist may have to adapt his or her design to the adaptive limits of the snake species under consideration. Most snakes are crepuscular (active at dawn and dusk) or nocturnal (active at night), so only a few species make interesting diurnal (daytime) displays. Although crepuscular snakes may be visible during the day, they usually are

An Irian Jaya carpet python (*Morelia spilota* sp.) in a naturalistic vivarium. Proper landscape, temperature, and humidity (80-90 percent) will determine how much time this species spends resting above ground.

inactive. The use of low-wattage, red incandescent bulbs at night will allow you to observe the activity and behaviors of many nocturnal snakes, including milk snakes, Trans Pecos rat snakes, house snakes, Pacific boas, and tree pythons and boas.

The three-fold challenge is meeting the needs of a species, creating a functional habitat, and making the system aesthetically appealing to the human observer. This is what makes the art of keeping snakes one of the most interesting and creative hobbies today.

CHAPTER 2:

BEFORE YOU BUY

U nfortunately, many uninformed people buy snakes for the wrong reasons. Snakes are wonderful creatures, but they are not a good choice if you want an expressive or personable pet. They lack facial expression and their lidless eyes are always open. They are solitary, antisocial creatures, exhibiting little or no responsiveness toward their owners. Long-term handling is stressful for many species.

The primary reward from owning snakes is not interactive but is instead derived from observing them in beautiful, carefully designed displays, somewhat like tropical fish. There is also a personal reward from caring for and trying to understand a creature that is so different from

Amazon tree boas *(Corallus hortulanus)* are a lot like some of the carpet pythons. They spend the day in shelters either at ground level or on raised shelves or thick branches. At night they are active and climb on tree branches.

ourselves. A type of knowledge and personal growth results from the process: a greater level of understanding and empathy for animals and possibly a sense of evolutionary history.

In today's busy world, snakes are practical pets. They demand less maintenance than most other animals. They don't require interaction, daily feeding (depending on the species and age), walks outdoors, litter boxes, or a lot of space. They are so undemanding that you can, with a clear conscience, leave your snake for a weekend or even an entire week without asking someone to take care of it.

Selection

There are five steps to selecting a species of snake:

1. Ask yourself why you want a snake and what you expect from it.
2. Research various snake species and select one that is likely to fill your needs.
3. Research the requirements and habits of the species you have considered.
4. Plan and design a vivarium for that species based on your research.
5. Carefully select and purchase one or more specimens for the vivarium you have designed.

Although rosy boas (*Lichanura trivirgata*) are sometimes considered dull and secretive, they will come out to bask in the open during the day and will climb on a variety of landscape structures when maintained in naturalistic vivaria.

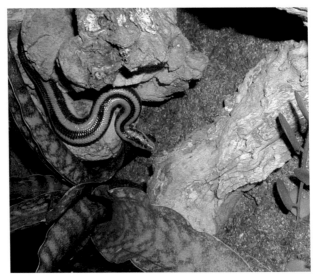

The above is the ideal sequence for selecting and buying a snake. Unfortunately, it's more typical for a person to buy a snake on impulse at a store or reptile show along with the LAM supplies recommended by the seller. It's no surprise that many of these owners eventually get rid of their snakes. They become disappointed and bored, and are no longer willing to dedicate the space, time, and effort to keeping them. Many short-term snake breeders get rid of their collections because the work involved in keeping large numbers of snakes in LAM conditions provides no pleasure and isn't justified by the marginal income.

Selecting a Species

As a snake keeper, no process is more important than the selection of species. Do not rush into buying a snake. Instead, give long and careful thought to your decision, asking yourself what it is you expect. Your selection will determine the size of the enclosure required, how the vivarium is designed, and the kind of relationship and aesthetic experience you will gain from owning a snake. The rule is: think, research, and then buy.

Research

Snake species differ significantly in terms of their body proportions, features, colors, habits, and behaviors. The best way to select a species is to look at live animals or photographs, read up on them, and ask questions of individuals who keep and breed them. People vary a great deal in the kinds of snakes they find appealing. Most people prefer heavy-bodied, slower-moving species that can be easily handled. A few are attracted to the sleek, slender, and fast-moving snakes, while others go for bright colors. Snake faces vary; dog-faced snakes, with broad heads and long snouts (like many of the boas and pythons) have wide appeal. Other hobbyists like snakes with rounded heads or large eyes.

If you have a chance, ask to handle a snake of the type you are considering to get a sense of its level of vigor, activity, and kinds of movements. Some snakes are edgy and jerky in their movements, wanting nothing more than to get away from you as quickly as possible. Others are slow moving and clingy. Scarlet kingsnakes and many of the milk snakes are beautifully colored but so secretive that they make poor display animals. Moreover, many milk snakes are restless and jerky in their movements. It is always a challenge to design a vivarium that allows regular viewing of these brightly colored snakes. Alternatively, rat snakes are not as attractive as milk snakes and are more restless and ready to bite than some species, but they are also more active and visually alert, making them more interesting displays. Many of the boas and pythons are beautiful with relatively calm demeanors, but some grow too large for most households while others are prone to biting. Finally, you must consider that most of the snakes available commercially feed on whole vertebrate prey, primarily mice and rats. Keeping these snakes forces you to confront the killing of other creatures, a requirement that many in modern, western cultures are uncomfortable with. The fact is, in addition to snakes, you will also be dealing with their prey—mice or rats, alive or dead.

Take the time to evaluate the species most suitable for you, and you will have not only a more rewarding snake-keeping experience but also a longer lasting one.

Size

Size does matter, and it is a critical consideration when buying snakes. As a rule, giant snakes, such as Burmese and reticulated pythons, are unsuitable for the great majority of prospective snake keepers. Most giant snakes, once they reach a certain size, either die from neglect or are given away because owners are no longer willing or able to keep or take proper care of them. Because of the special considerations in their selection, care, housing, and handling, the giant snakes are not covered in this book. Large snakes (6 to 9 feet), such as most boa constrictors, carpet pythons, spilotes, and indigo snakes, are more manageable but still require cages at least 6 feet long and 18 inches wide when adult. If you can afford the space, these large, impressive species make attention-grabbing displays. However, better suited for most households are the medium-sized snakes (up to 6 feet), such as rat snakes, kingsnakes, and smaller boas and pythons that can survive in cages 48 to 60 inches long when adult.

Habits

Many snakes are uncomfortable spending extended periods of time in the open during the day; a great number of them are crepuscular or nocturnal. If your goal is to have a snake that is visible during the day, you will have to pay special attention to selecting a species that doesn't mind resting in the open instead of hiding inside a shelter.

Good open-display species are:
- Tree dwellers such as green tree pythons, carpet pythons, or green red-tailed rat snakes;
- Semiarboreal species such as Russian rat snakes;
- Diurnal ground dwellers such as diadem snakes.

Crepuscular and nocturnal species are visible during the day only if shelters are specially designed to provide a view of the coiled, resting snake.

Behaviors

Snakes vary in their speed of motion, type of movement, degree of restlessness, tendency to writhe, ability to learn, and propensity for fight or flight, striking and biting, and releasing foul-smelling musk. They also differ in their tolerance of handling.

Behavioral tendencies are what give a snake its character profile, something you can only know from observation and handling. Most boas and pythons, for example, tend to move slowly and, unless frightened, avoid falling, so they are easily handled. On the other hand, water snakes are restless, tend to writhe, release a foul-smelling musk, and will readily fall to the ground, making them poor candidates for handling. The behavior patterns of snakes play a role not only in terms of handling but also in the kinds of activities they perform in a vivarium and their value as display snakes. Snakes that are poor candidates for handling, such

All members of the genus *Candoia* are secretive and nocturnal but if offered open-faced shelters, Solomon island ground boas can be observed sleeping during the day.

as water snakes, can make excellent display species because they will come into the open and bask during the day. Their propensity for swimming or spending time submerged in a water container also has interesting display benefits.

Selecting Healthy Individuals

Probably the most important factor in longevity is choosing a healthy snake. Avoiding snakes that are ill or that require an extended period of time to establish in captivity is critical in your enjoyment of an animal and its long-term survival.

When possible, buy young, half-grown snakes. Half-grown snakes usually feed well so you will not have to deal with the feeding problems sometimes associated with babies or juveniles. Buying half-grown snakes also gives you a general idea of a snake's age: its age can be more or less ascertained by comparisons with the growth rate of captive specimens. With imported snakes, smaller, immature specimens often acclimate better to captive conditions than older, mature specimens. They are also less likely to be heavily parasitized.

Get the idea of nursing or saving a sick or mistreated snake out of your head. Sick snakes can be expensive and tedious to treat and are best left to experts. Very sick snakes are probably best euthanized. Moreover, they are a health risk to the other snakes in your collection.

Wild-Caught versus Captive-Bred

With most snakes, buying captive-bred individuals is preferable to purchasing wild-collected ones. Wild-caught snakes often harbor parasites and require an acclimation period before they adjust to captive conditions. Some wild-collected snakes also harbor bacteria or viruses that can threaten other snakes in an existing collection. Don't buy wild-caught snakes unless it is the only way to obtain the species you desire or the captive-bred specimens are prohibitively expensive. It is very difficult to acclimate wild-caught snakes to captivity. Fortunately, a wide variety of snakes are now bred in captivity and are readily available to prospective snake buyers.

Steps to Choosing a Healthy Pet

Observe the snake in its cage. It should be active or coiled. Look for external signs of thinness, such as a pronounced backbone or asymmetry of appearance—a body section that shows swelling or collapse or an eye that is smaller than the other.

Check for kinks in the backbone and tail, and for depressions in the rib cage. These signs indicate broken bones.

Examine the mouth. The edges of the mouth should be flush when it is closed. If an edge sticks out because of some apparent swelling, there is a good chance that the snake has stomatitis, a bacterial infection of the gums.

Check the skin. It must be free of injuries, bumps, and areas of raised scales or blisters.

Check for mites. These tiny external parasites appear like crawling little black beads on the skin, or they can be seen as a tiny, raised edge when lodged in the corners of the eyes. Tiny white flecks on the snake's body are a good indicator of mites. These are usually mite feces. When holding a snake, check for mites by allowing the snake's body to run between your fingers and hand. Then check your hand for crawling mites or blood streaks from crushed mites.

Check for alertness and vigor. A snake with good weight that is active in its cage and regularly flicks its tongue as it moves is probably healthy. Snakes that are coiled in a shelter or a cage corner are probably resting or sleeping. The only way to make sure a snake is vigorous is to ask the seller to allow you to handle it or to show you how the snake moves in its cage or in his or her hands. Healthy snakes give a clear impression of strength and vigor when in hand. Avoid snakes that look or feel weak and limp.

Check for respiratory infection. Gently press up on the underside of the throat and check to see if any bubbly mucus emerges from the sides of the mouth or the nostrils; this is a sign of respiratory infection. Gaping and forced exhalations are other signs of respiratory disease.

Look at the underside of the snake. The belly scales should be flush with the body, with no signs of swelling between scales. The belly should not have brown or reddish discolored areas, or scales that appear raised or ragged as if the edges were chewed. These are all signs of possible skin or systemic bacterial infections. The anal scale(s) should rest flush with the base of the tail. There should be no crusting or fecal smears around the vent (anus). A swollen or crusted vent and fecal smears are signs of parasites or bacterial infections.

Look for signs of neurological problems. It is always a good idea to watch a snake move, either in its cage or when handled, looking for odd behaviors that indicate neurological disorders or diseases. Behaviors include raising the front part of the body then flopping over and down, or jerky side-to-side movements as if the snake can't keep its balance. Avoid any snakes that demonstrate signs of uncoordinated behaviors.

Do a general exam. Allow the snake to run through your hand, your fingers lifted against the middle of the belly. With light pressure, palpate for lumps or hard masses. Recently swallowed food will feel like a soft lump around the middle of the body. In ovulating females, the mature, rounded ova feel like small marbles. In terms of health, feel for large, hard masses. For example, one recently obtained young hognose snake had an enlarged posterior abdominal area and when run through the fingers, a hard, elongated mass could be felt. The snake ate but produced only small feces. The hard mass remained in place and was typical of intestinal blockage or possibly a tumor. Had the snake been examined prior to purchase, the hassle and cost of its medical problem would have been avoided.

Experienced hobbyists and veterinarians can evaluate the location, shape, and hardness of a mass to determine possible problems, such as constipation, egg binding, blockages, or tumors.

Speaking in Tongues

Snakes have expressionless faces, so you must evaluate their state of health or behavioral intent from their behaviors and body postures. For example, most snakes form an S-like coil with the front part of the body prior to a strike. Various species also perform defensive displays in response to a perceived threat, such as the raised, hooded display of spectacled cobras. There is one behavior that, although subtle, can indicate a snake's psychological state—tongue flicks.

When the snake flicks its tongue, the tongue extends out of the mouth, picks up chemical cues from the surrounding environment, and then transfers the chemicals to a sensory organ at the roof of the mouth called Jacobson's organ. This sensory organ, in coordination with sensory-interpretation areas of the brain, generates a

Indonesian dwarf ground boas *(Candoia carinata carinata)* spend most of the day concealed either under shelters or between the stacked leaves of plants, such as dracaenas, bromeliads, or birds nest sansevieria.

unique type of taste-smell. To a significant degree, the rate of tongue flicking reflects the level of interest a snake has in its surrounding environment. Sick, weak snakes have little interest in the surrounding environment and typically perform few tongue flicks. Very sick snakes do not perform tongue flicks unless awakened from their stupor and even then the flick rate is reduced and slower.

When snakes find chemical cues interesting or exciting, the rate of tongue-flicks increases. This can be readily observed when a snake inspects a dead mouse prior to performing the snout-rubbing behavior to ascertain the location of the prey's head (the direction of hair growth and hardness of the skull allows a snake to recognize the position of the prey's head). Many snakes also demonstrate high tongue-flick rates when courting females during the breeding season. At that time, the scent of freshly shed female snakes is so stimulating to males that they can't quite believe their tongues and flick over and over again. A snake, when exploring a new environment, performs a steady rate of tongue flicking as it moves. An area of interest will cause it to stop and spend time tongue checking. On the other hand, when frightened and wary, or when assuming a defensive display, many snakes perform a low rate of extended tongue flicks, the tongue lingering out of the mouth and sometimes waving up and down. In some snakes, the tongue is brightly colored orange-red or, in the case of red-tailed rat snakes, vivid blue and black. These colorful tongues may be extended or waved up and down when faced with prey, possibly to act as a lure, as well as during defensive behaviors.

CHAPTER 3:

QUARANTINE AND INTRODUCTION TO VIVARIA

To ensure the health of an existing collection, there is nothing you can do that is more important than quarantining new arrivals—keeping them singly and in isolation. Captive-bred or captive-raised snakes should be quarantined individually for at least thirty days. Wild-caught snakes should be quarantined for a minimum of sixty days before introduction to a naturalistic vivarium.

When using naturalistic vivaria, treating mites and other diseases requires dismantling the entire setup, so it's best to catch any problems before introducing a new snake to its home—even if it will be kept singly.

Quarantine tanks should be simply designed LAM setups, with paper as a substrate (except for burrowing species such as sand boas), a shelter, a water dish, and, for arboreal species, appropriate perching areas. With captive-bred and -raised species that have good weight, carefully examine snakes for signs of mites or treat them prophylactically by using an ivermectin spray. During the quarantine period, offer food to the snake and observe at least two fecal droppings. The droppings should be semiformed or formed, and dark with whitish urates. Snakes that fail to feed readily or pass discolored, bloody, runny, or unusually smelly stools should have a fecal exam for parasites and be evaluated by a qualified veterinarian. Monitor snakes for other signs of disease, such as gaping, forced exhalations, swellings of the mouth, and neurological problems. If a snake has good weight, is captive-bred and -raised, and is the only snake being introduced to the vivarium, a four-week quarantine period is adequate.

Quarantine captive-bred and -raised boa constrictors as described above, but subsequently house them individually because of the risks of inclusion body disease (IBD), a viral disease of certain boid snakes that is somewhat analogous to AIDS (IBD is caused by a retrovirus and is transmitted through copulation or blood-associated vectors. The disease depresses the immune system, and it can take months or even years before its symptoms become obvious.). If interested in mixing boa constrictors for display or for breeding, a liver biopsy to assess the possible presence of the IBD virus should be performed about six months after purchase. If you are seriously considering breeding boa constrictors, checking for IBD is a must. Boas with IBD can live for several years without showing any signs of the disease, so quarantine is not an effective method for revealing its presence. If you are keeping a single boa constrictor, even if IBD infected, there is a good chance you will have it for several years and it should not cause any problems as long as it is isolated and you adhere to common-sense hygienic procedures.

Wild-Caught Snakes

Imported snakes generally present a much greater risk of disease, so they require longer quarantine—at least sixty days. All wild-collected snakes should be evaluated for external parasites, and internal parasites, through a fecal exam, and then treated as needed. Viperid snakes (vipers and pit vipers) are notorious as sources of paramyxovirus— a deadly respiratory virus—but it can also infect other species, notably several of the Asian rat snakes. Viperids should be quarantined in rooms or buildings completely separate from an existing collection. Monitor feeding responses and weight changes.

While in quarantine, pay close attention to the presence of mites or ticks, or treat the snakes prophylactically with an ivermectin spray. Because there is a high risk of a crash (a sudden, usually terminal, decline in health) within the first few weeks in captivity, hobbyists should be very attentive to signs of possible disease, such as runny, discolored (pale), or smelly feces; skin infections; weight loss; gaping and forced exhalations; inactivity; lack of muscular vigor; or neurological signs. As you notice problems, attempt to diagnose the cause and treat accordingly. Consult a qualified reptile veterinarian during the quarantine and acclimation period.

If you are inexperienced with acclimating wild-collected snakes—particularly tropical species—you will find it much more economical and satisfying to start off with captive-bred specimens. The mortality rate of many imported snakes often exceeds 50 percent during the first six months in captivity, so even paying two or more times the price of an imported snake for a captive-bred specimen ends up being a bargain. Boa constrictors are an exception because a significant percentage of individuals in captivity may be infected with the IBD virus.

Introducing Snakes into the Vivarium

After quarantine, transfer the snake from a simple, bare enclosure to the more stimulating and complex environment of a naturalistic vivarium. The snake's reaction to the environmental change will communicate how well the snake is adapting to the display environment and guide you in the design changes necessary to accommodate its requirements.

When you introduce a snake into a new vivarium, you will observe one of three patterns of behavior: the snake will rush for the nearest accessible shelter and hide, go into a hyperactive frenzy trying to find any possible means of escape, or undertake a calm exploratory tour of the cage.

Most snakes require about a week, sometimes several weeks, before they settle in and develop behavior routines. For example, my corn snake spent most its first week hiding, but eventually established patterns—it comes out to bask in the morning for several hours before retiring into its shelter for most of the day, then emerges again in the early evening. My radiated rat snakes invariably come out and climb to a raised basking site in the early afternoon to take advantage of the sunlight that lights the upper part of their setup.

During the initial stages of introduction, snakes will test all of the landscape components. Structures that are not anchored properly will fall and some plants may be crushed or damaged. As a result, you may need to do some rearrangement after the snakes have settled in. Take advantage of periods when the snakes are resting in their shelters so you don't bother them when you make changes in the vivarium. In addition to securing or removing structures that have toppled, you may decide to change part of the landscape or add landscape features based on your snake's behaviors. Major changes in enclosure design require that you temporarily remove the snake. In the first weeks following setup, I usually transfer my snakes to a temporary storage container at least a couple of times in order to make changes to the landscape design.

Traditional Care of Snakes: LAM

Many snakes are currently kept and displayed in the most functionally efficient method possible, in a manner very similar to laboratory rodents. This method was initially developed by importers and commercial dealers, then later expanded by breeders who needed to maintain large numbers of animals with the most space- and labor-efficient method possible. The LAM method is similar to the maintenance techniques used for small animals, such as hamsters and gerbils, and the maintenance of confined production farm animals. The LAM method may have practical applications for commercial breeding, research, or systems of temporary housing (such as for quarantining individual snakes). Nevertheless, the pragmatism of the moment should be weighed against the health and well being of snakes kept as sentient animals in naturalistic vivaria.

The basic LAM setup is simple. Place a snake in a secure aerated box or screen-covered tank. Add a layer of wood shavings, either pine or preferably aspen. Put in a smaller box with a hole as a shelter and add a water dish. Provide a hot spot using either a subtank heating unit or an overhead, infrared heat source at one end of the enclosure to create a heat gradient. Feed every seven to ten days. Change water weekly or when fouled. Replace the substrate every one to three weeks. That's all there is to it. Many snakes will live and breed for years under these conditions, and you will have as much enjoyment keeping a snake as you would a laboratory mouse.

CHAPTER 4:

LIFE STAGES AND HUSBANDRY

As humans, we readily recognize the importance of our different life stages and adjust our behaviors accordingly. We know that babies have different requirements than five year olds and that adolescents have a different worldview than mature adults. Some of these differences are subtle, but others are more drastic and correspond to a shift of niche in human society. For example, the helpless baby, unable to walk or talk and dependent on its parents to fulfill its needs, occupies a markedly different dietary and social niche than an adolescent.

Because of their smaller size, baby snakes often have different requirements and occupy a different ecological niche than adults. For example, in the wild, most rat

This baby Andesian milk snake *(Lampropeltis triangulum andesiana)* initially spent time exploring its cage. Later, it burrowed in the substrate and did what milk snakes typically do: hid and became invisible.

snakes, kingsnakes, and smaller boids—which as adults feed primarily on warm-blooded prey—start off feeding on cold-blooded prey, such as lizards and amphibians. Babies' shelter requirements, preferred activity areas, and periods of activity are also markedly different than adults'. Adjusting the size and design of a vivarium so that they can meet the needs of different life stages is a necessary consideration when applying the principles of the art of keeping snakes. So, how do we categorize the life stages of snakes?

In an article I published in *Vivarium* magazine (1999), along with Susan Donoghue, V.M.D., and Roger Klingenberg, D.V.M., I introduced the importance of development and life stages in the husbandry of reptiles and amphibians, presenting a simple categorization of life stages as follows:

1. Prebirth/embryonic stage: This stage is spent inside the egg or body of the mother, depending on the species.
2. Presexual: From hatchling/neonate to adult, the presexual stage is characterized by a high growth rate. This stage can be broken down into two substages: juvenile and subadult.
3. Reproductive adult: This stage is triggered by the production of sex hormones and the maturation of sex organs. It is characterized by a tapering off of growth rate and the onset of reproductive behaviors. This stage can be broken down into two substages: early sexual maturity and advanced sexual maturity.
4. Old age: This stage is characterized in many species by little to no growth, decrease in shedding frequency, and little to no reproduction.

As an example of how husbandry must address life stages, we know that with many species of snake increased feeding regimens during the presexual stage can increase initial growth rate and lead to early sexual maturity. We also know that with older snakes the same intensive feeding regimen that led to a high growth rate for younger snakes can lead to obesity and shorter life. In many species, life stages are also associated with changes in niche (ecological role, diet, and area or time of activity). Some snakes are terrestrial and feed primarily on amphibians and reptiles when young but switch to a more arboreal habit and feed primarily on warm-blooded prey when older.

The design of a vivarium must accommodate the progression of life stages. Baby snakes that use small shelters require larger shelters as they get older; snakes that when young perched on twigs require thick branches as adults. Landscape structures and plants that can bear the activity of small snakes are replaced with sturdier plants for adults. Basking sites and the associated heating units must also be adjusted.

To raise baby snakes, many snake keepers prefer the closer monitoring possibilities provided by LAM setups but switch to a naturalistic display approach by the time the snakes are subadults.

CHAPTER 5:

DESIGN PLANNING

One of the goals of keeping snakes in captivity is having the opportunity to observe them. Rather than cater exclusively to a snake's needs, a hobbyist usually attempts to create a design that achieves a balance between the snake's requirements and an appealing composition. Ultimately, the design and landscaping of a vivarium makes the difference between a dull, functional display and one that brings enjoyment and invites regular viewing. A well-planned design will not only make a setup more attractive but will also make it more interesting for the snake(s) maintained. To use a term commonly used in the zoo community, it will "enrich the captive environment" of the snake and invite a greater range of behaviors.

Vivaria Shape Behaviors

Vivaria are not replicas of nature, in part because the materials required to replicate nature are unavailable or unaffordable. The general goal for naturalistic vivarium

Radiated rat snakes *(Elaphe radiata)* proved outstanding displays in the author's setups, spending parts of the day on raised rest areas basking under lights or in sunlight reaching the tank.

34

design is to simulate the essential aspects of the natural habitat required by a species within an enclosure. For example, you may not be able to provide the specific tree upon which emerald tree boas coil in the Amazon forest, but you can come up with landscape structures that will simulate the characteristics of those trees, such as horizontal branches, appropriate branch diameter, and bark texture. You cannot reproduce the sun but you can provide those aspects of sunlight required by a snake, such as light and heat, through artificial lighting.

Because the essential aspects of a snake's natural habitat can be simulated in different ways, there are a variety of possible design approaches to meet the requirements of different snake species. In addition, snakes have adaptive potential and adaptive plasticity; they are not rigidly programmed biological automata. A vivarium design, although different than what they would encounter in nature, will generally test the adaptive capabilities of snakes and shape their behaviors. The failure of a species or individual to adapt is generally manifested through hyper-activity, failure to form behavior routines, poor feeding, weight loss, and possibly disease and death.

The behavior-shaping features of vivarium design are easily tested. Take, for example, a rat snake. Put it in a bare tank and only include a broad section of wood running diagonally from the bottom of one side to the top of the opposite side of the tank. That piece of wood will serve as an attractor and draw the snake toward it. The snake will investigate the wood, climb on it, and, if a light is placed above a section of the wood, probably use it as a basking site. If the wood is broad enough at ground level, the rat snake may decide to coil underneath it, using it as shelter. The snake will adapt its behaviors in relation to the wood. In nature and vivaria with varied topography, snakes investigate their environments and adapt their behaviors to the range of opportunities presented, including heat sources, light, perching areas, shelters, and food availability.

A rule of design is that, within certain limits, the topography of a vivarium shapes snake behavior. A good

vivarist creates designs that have visual impact and optimize the opportunities for observing snakes. Taking the above factors into consideration, there are three steps to designing a vivarium for snakes.

Research

You will not be able to design a vivarium without information on a species' requirements, habits, and essential aspects of its natural habitat. For example, putting a rosy boa—a species from arid areas—in a humid, lushly planted tropical vivarium will eventually cause skin and respiratory problems that lead to its death.

The first step in vivarium design is to research the species you wish to maintain, its natural habitat, the plants you are considering for the setup, and the materials and technology available.

Planning

Good design requires planning. An artist usually starts off with a general vision of his or her goal, but that vision will be altered and modified in the process of actualization. Nonetheless, general vision determines the design theme: what materials need to be purchased and how much material will be used. This rough plan will in part result from your initial research on the snake's behavioral propensities and its habitat. Jot down your ideas on a piece of paper and sketch a rough design. Then, make a list of the supplies that will be needed to accomplish the task.

Improvisation and Flexibility

After you have obtained all the supplies for creating a snake vivarium, the process of assembly requires some improvisation. The actualization seldom matches what has been drawn on paper and usually new possibilities come to mind during the course of assembly. The aesthetics and balance of the composition may require you to step back, evaluate, and change or adjust. No matter what your completed vivarium looks like, the initial design will always be experimental, because you cannot completely predict the behaviors of the individual snake you introduce to the setup. During the first few days or weeks of introduction you will have to make adjustments to accommodate the behaviors of the snake. Some structures may end up toppled over; some plants may be damaged. It is also possible that the landscaping doesn't meet the requirements of the snake and it may exhibit prolonged signs of stress. In most cases, your design will require some changes no matter how good you think it is.

Adjustment Period

A vivarium challenges the adaptive plasticity of snakes and shapes a snake's behavior patterns. As a result, there is a period of time, usually several weeks, before a snake has fully adapted to the vivarium environment and established behavior patterns in relation to it. After an initial investigation of the setup, it is not uncommon for a snake to spend an extended period of time in a shelter. Eventually, the snake will come out for increasing periods of time.

The best evidence of a well-designed setup is the readiness with which a snake settles in and establishes behavior patterns. The clues to adaptation are in fact the formation of daily patterns of activity. For example, a snake basks on a section of log in the morning and retires at midday to spend time in its preferred shelter, then emerges for basking in the late afternoon. Broader patterns may also be formed, particularly around the shedding cycle when snakes may soak in water dishes or remain concealed in a shelter or buried in substrate. A badly designed setup will cause a snake to display signs of stress, such as hyperactivity, long-term inactivity, poor feeding, weight loss, and disease. The conditions within a vivarium, from landscaping to light and heat levels, must be carefully examined and revised when a snake shows obvious signs of stress or maladaption.

CHAPTER 6:

ENCLOSURES AND BACKGROUNDS

T he first step to housing a snake is selecting an enclosure that meets the essential requirements of the species that you intend to keep, and that is appropriate for the space you have available and the design you have in mind.

An enclosure should be large enough for a snake to perform a range of behaviors, including basking and finding shelters, but not so large that the snake cannot be observed and monitored. In addition, a snake cage should be secure when closed, with a locking mechanism to prevent escapes.

The Best Snake Enclosures

From a practical standpoint, the best snake enclosures have a sliding-glass front, screen top, and a deep, watertight

The author's radiated rat snake setup has a back wall of cultured rock. The rock was siliconed to the back of the tank and provides ledges and a rough surface to aid shedding.

bottom. Sliding-glass front doors allow for easy maintenance of the enclosure without removal of the lights resting on top. There are several companies that manufacture plastic-sided enclosures with glass fronts (Bush and Vision Herpetological), which can be purchased at reptile stores. Melamine and wood cages with sliding or hinged glass fronts are attractive but will not work with the methods presented here because they do not hold water; both melamine and wood swell and warp when wet.

The most readily available and inexpensive reptile enclosures in the pet trade are all-glass tanks with sliding screen tops. These work well with smaller and ground-dwelling snakes but are problematic with larger snakes and arboreal species. Top-opening tanks larger than 20 inches tall are too tall for most people to reach the bottom for routine maintenance. For larger arboreal snakes requiring tall enclosures, use vivaria with a front or side access.

No matter what kind of enclosure you purchase, it should always have a locking mechanism, whether a pin (sliding screen tops), a latch and lock, or a cabinet-lock (sliding-glass fronts). The first rule of responsible snake keeping is to have an escape-proof enclosure.

Snakes should always be kept in secure cages with some type of locking mechanism. Sliding-front cages can usually be secured with cabinet locks.

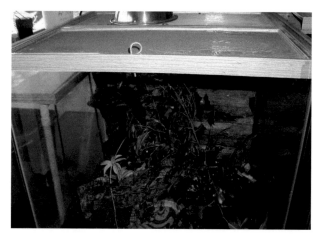

The sliding screen-top cages that are so popular in the hobby can be secured with a pin-type lock.

Enclosure Size

The principles underlying the art of keeping snakes require larger minimum enclosure sizes than what is recommended by the LAM method. With the LAM method, the minimum enclosure size for keeping reptiles is humane but constraining. The full range of snake behaviors will not be expressed in small, sterile cages. Small enclosure size and minimum landscaping play a key role in the perception that snakes are dull creatures. Given adequate space, you will observe a much broader behavioral repertoire and greater levels of responsive behaviors. Small enclosures limit environment-related behaviors, exploratory behavior, territorial behavior, and owner-related behavior. For some species of reptiles, small enclosures tend to elicit what I call "cornered behaviors" in relationship to outside stimuli. When faced with a human observer, they display fight or flight behaviors.

If your interest is in the art of keeping snakes, then use a large enclosure, with a perimeter at least two and one-half times the total length of the animals—preferably three times their total length. If you plan to keep a semiarboreal or arboreal species, the enclosure height should be at least 50 percent of the total length of the snake.

Tall Enclosures: Give careful thought to the height of enclosures. Tall enclosures are attractive but present certain

A banded wart snake in the author's 2- by 4-foot setup. This species, like many other aquatic snakes, makes a great display.

problems. For ground-dwelling species, such as many desert snakes, tall enclosure are difficult to light and heat because they require high-wattage sources to adequately warm ground-level basking sites and provide light to plants. As a rule, enclosures with top access that are more than 20 inches tall are difficult to maintain because you cannot readily reach the bottom. With species that require tall enclosures, use front-opening tanks.

Backgrounds

The dedicated snake vivarist gives attention to the details of each stage of vivarium design, including the background. The most simple background for a vivarium is a solid color that complements the design components. Black backgrounds are probably the most effective in creating a dramatic contrast with landscape structures and light-colored or brightly colored snakes. Paint the back of the tank with black spray paint or latex paint. Some custom enclosure manufacturers provide black acrylic or black glass backgrounds. As an alternative, a pale blue background simulates the color of the sky and can be very effective in providing contrast with the color of most snakes and the interior components of a setup. You can paint the back of the tank with a light blue latex paint or apply a sky blue acrylic backing to create this effect.

Some vivarists strive for a purely artistic effect without concern to whether the setup appears natural. For example, one vivarist wanted to emphasize a white theme: the enclosure was custom-made and painted white, the background was white, the substrate was white sand, the shelter was white, and the perching wood was painted white, as were a couple of artificial plants. In the display was a pair of leucistic Texas rat snakes—solid white snakes with blue white irises.

Or, as another example, you can choose an Australian theme, like the vivarium once designed by artist and herpetoculturist Russ Gurley. In this design the background was made of molded concrete stained a rich gray red color to simulate a rock wall. A section of an old aboriginal wall painting was reproduced on the background using acrylic paint and red sand was placed on the bottom of the tank along with stacked rocks and a pair of Australian spotted pythons *(Antaresia childreni)*. In both examples, the background was customized to complement the theme of the design.

Cultured Stone and Cork Bark

Cultured stone is a term for man-made sections of lightweight concrete, molded and stained to simulate real stone. It is available from businesses that specialize in stone and tile. Good quality cultured stone is difficult to tell apart from walls or other structures made of real stone. Very attractive backgrounds can be made by siliconing cultured stone sections to the back of enclosures. Another alternative for creating a rich, natural-looking textured background is to glue natural cork bark sections or cork bark tiles to the back of the enclosure. Both cultured stone and natural cork bark create three-dimensional backgrounds that are quite effective and add visual complexity to the vivarium. Both also provide activity and climbing surfaces for snakes.

CHAPTER 7:

SUBSTRATES

I t's time to decide on a substrate for your vivarium. The substrate (the medium your animal lives on) is one of the most important components in the design of a captive environment. Your animal will lie, move, and defecate on the substrate, and will often feed on it, as well. With the LAM system, substrate theory focuses on the moisture absorption potential of the substrate, relative safety if ingested, cost, ease of handling, and texture suitable for burrowing. This is why wood shavings, particularly low-phenol (little resin smell) pine and aspen, are the most used and recommended substrates by commercial snake breeders.

Using the naturalistic approach initially advocated by European herpetoculturists such as Ludwig Trutnau (1986), select substrates that give a natural appearance. These range from fine gravel, sand, and sand/soil mixes for species from desert areas to fir bark, soil mixes, and leaf litter for species from tropical forests. With the naturalistic approach, the standard method of maintenance is to

If kept on a moist substrate with areas partially covered by foliage overhead, the viper boa *(Candoia aspera)* will be visible as a display animal.

regularly scoop out the fecal material and replace parts of the substrate as needed. Most substrates used with ground-dwelling snakes should have a dry surface, because prolonged contact with a moist substrate can lead to bacterial infections of the skin.

A Revolution in Substrates: The Bioactive Substrate System

The ideal substrate for keeping and displaying snakes should look natural and attractive, allow for easy maintenance, have longevity, and require infrequent replenishment, while still allowing you to keep animals and plants healthy and the vivarium free of bad odors and unsightly waste. The Bioactive Substrate System (BSS) that I developed is a revolutionary method for keeping snakes and other reptiles. It offers all of the ideal substrate qualities.

The method allows you to keep snakes on a natural-looking substrate that bioactively processes waste residues and allows for the growth of live plants, accomplishing the goals of the art of keeping snakes. The key to the BSS system is the colonization by beneficial aerobic bacteria, which break down the waste residue of snakes and other animals.

Origins of the BSS

The idea of developing bioactive substrates for keeping snakes resulted from research with a different kind of reptile. Early in 2000, I decided to transfer my original pair of New Caledonian giant geckos *(Rhacodactylus leachianus)* to a larger tank. As I removed the bark and soil from their original tank, I noticed that the substrate had a nice, rich, earthy smell to it and had the texture of high-quality humus. It occurred to me that the substrate had not been changed in nearly three years because it never smelled or looked dirty. This was the same substrate that these geckos defecated in and laid their eggs in. The substrate was misted daily and stirred three times a week when I looked for eggs.

I did some research to find out what allowed the substrate to acquire this rich, odorless quality and discovered it was bacterial bioactivity and the same sort of dispersed composting (versus the concentrated composting in compost piles) that occurs in nature. I wondered whether the same principle could be applied to keeping other herps.

One of the first experiments I performed was with banded water snakes, a species considered particularly messy and smelly to keep. I had been working for over five years to establish an albino strain of banded water snakes and maintained a number of specimens. Changing their messy and smelly newspaper substrate every week was a chore, so I switched them to an experimental substrate mix, placing them on 2½ inches of moist mix. Instead of replacing paper, all I did was remove fecal masses from the surface and then stir the substrate once a week so any surface waste was blended with the deeper, moist bacterial layer. One concern I had with keeping water snakes on a moist substrate was the dreaded skin blister disease associated with bacterial infections of the skin. This did not happen. After a few weeks, I evaluated the substrate using the smell test. The cage had no significant odor except a mild, sweet, earthy smell. Eleven months later, the substrate was still functional with no significant smell.

Another interesting thing was that the water snakes displayed behaviors in relation to the substrate, such as partial burrowing, that I had not noticed before. The experiment was so encouraging that I switched all of my

Water snakes are among the most enjoyable snakes to keep and observe in naturalistic setups. They are generally more active during the day than most snakes, in part because they're diurnal visual hunters.

The author mixes different proportions of one or more of the following in his substrate mix: peat moss or a peat moss-based potting soil; sand; fine-grade fir bark, such as orchid bark; a fired clay, such as bentonite clay (unscented fired clay cat litter); and a fine-grade black scoria (lava rock).

snakes to bioactive substrates, including my rat snakes, kingsnakes, boas, and pythons. As suspected, I had the same satisfying results. These experiments and others radically changed my thinking about herpetoculture and vivarium design and have led me to conclude that most current substrate theory in herpetoculture, usually involving substrate products that provide a pet rodent approach to keeping snakes (with an emphasis on absorption of moisture and reduced biological activity), is flawed.

What is a Bioactive Substrate?

A substrate that has active bacteria and other micro-organisms, including algae, fungi, protozoa, and soil nema-todes, is said to be bioactive, meaning it contains biological agents that perform work. The primary and most important activity is performed by bacteria. The bacteria colonize surfaces of substrate components, such as sand or clay, and form what are called biofilms, surface coatings of bacteria. If substrates become bioactive and biofilmed, their feel or texture changes. They end up filmy, almost silky, as a result of the bacterial or algal coating of particles and gel-like extracellular secretions by bacteria. An effect of this coating is that bioactive substrates aggregate and, unlike other freshly moistened soils, usually do not readily stick to the skin of snakes and other herps.

The bacteria that perform the kind of waste processing we want to occur in a vivarium substrate are aerobic heterotrophs, that is, they require oxygen and obtain their nutrients from other organic molecules, either from dead or living organisms. They also require a level of moisture and a source of nutrients. In vivaria that house snakes, waste matter with nitrogenous compounds is a source of food for nitrifying bacteria, which convert ammonia and nitrites to nitrates. To maintain the proper conditions for aerobic bacteria, the substrate must be aerated; meaning air must be able to penetrate between bacteria-covered particles.

In the vivarium, elements that are porous and non-compacting help aerate the substrate, retain moisture, and provide surface areas for bacterial activity. In the BSS system, these features are provided by volcanic rock, kiln-fired clays, or ceramics. To provide enough surface area for biofilms and for drainage, incorporate some type of sand or unfired clay into the mix. To assure moisture retention and to supply an additional source of organic material peat moss, include coir (ground coconut husk), ground fir bark, leaf litter, or ground moss, depending on the type of mix. Because soil bacteria grow best in a slightly alkaline substrate, add ground oyster shell or dolomite until the substrate has a pH of 7.4-8. You can purchase soil pH measuring kits though a local nursery or hardware store.

Depth and Watering of the Substrate

Whether you purchase a commercially formulated bioactive substrate for snakes or make your own, the depth of the substrate is important. If too shallow, the substrate will quickly dry out and be subject to alternating wet and dry cycles. To reduce the risk of drying out, use a minimum substrate depth of at least 2½ inches, preferably 3 to 4 inches. Use an enclosure with at least one glass side so you can monitor substrate moisture. Substrates dry out from the top down, so a glass-sided enclosure will allow you to monitor the drying process. As the top layer dries out, it becomes lighter in color than the darker, lower layer of substrate that still contains significant amounts of water. Allow some drying down to the top third of the substrate because the dry surface simulates nature. However, if the substrate dries completely it will cause either the death of bacteria or their inactivity through spore formation. Allowing the top part to dry, then wetting the substrate and stirring it encourages the bacteria to quickly recolonize.

Too much water will also reduce oxygen availability and will lead to the death of aerobic bacteria and cause an anaerobic bacteria surge—a sudden proliferation of one or several bacteria species. (Aerobic bacteria are bacteria that require or are able to use oxygen. Anaerobic bacteria are bacteria that require or are able to survive in anoxic, low oxygen, conditions.) When wet anaerobic conditions are generated, the substrate typically ends up stinking because of the death of aerobic organisms, the rise in anaerobic bacteria, and, later, the release of hydrogen sulfide.

Substrate Temperature

Optimal bacterial activity occurs at between 68 degrees Fahrenheit (F) and 95° F. With most snake species, strive for vivaria ground temperatures between 72° F and 82° F. Connect soil heating cables and subtank heaters to rheostats or thermostats to keep the substrate within the desired temperature range. Thermometers with probes that can be inserted into the substrate are ideal for measuring substrate temperature. As a rule, avoid substrate temperatures in the high 80s and 90s F, because they fail to provide the range of temperature gradients required by most snakes and they increase the water evaporation rate, quickly drying the substrate. In areas of the enclosure where the substrate temperature exceeds 95° F, expect bacterial death.

Scooping and Stirring: Activating Substrate

Bacteria reproduce quickly, with a generation measured in minutes or hours. Still, even after the substrate is inoculated with residues of waste matter, other factors, including initial competition with fungi, the amount of nutrients available, and proper pH and temperature, are required for extensive

There are three important maintenance procedures when using bioactive substrates. The first is to scoop out fecal masses from the surface of the substrate.

After fecal matter is removed, stir the substrate. A large plastic serving fork, works well. Make sure there are no snakes in the substrate before performing this procedure.

Weekly watering of the substrate and plants is an important part of maintaining a healthy bioactive substrate.

colonization by beneficial bacteria. With larger reptiles, there are two steps for activating the substrate. First, scoop the fecal mass (the bulk of the feces) off the surface to limit the amount of waste being processed. Next, and this is a critical step, stir the substrate to blend the top layers with the moist lower bioactive layers and distribute nutrients throughout the substrate. Depending on their composition, these nutrients will become available to plants and bacteria. In setups with low animal density, the bacterial load is able to keep up with the breakdown of fecal residues from the time of setup. A greater period of time will be required if there is a high animal density, six or more weeks depending on a number of factors (number and weight of animals, feeding frequency, temperature, and stirring).

One way to test for bioactivity is to send a substrate sample to one of the companies that test soil for bacterial counts—aim for more than a million bacteria per gram of substrate. An alternative test is to monitor manually for substrate aggregation and sliminess. In the early stages the substrate may cling to a snake's body but once it is bioactive it has a silky feel and particles tend to clump together, with little to none clinging to the snake's skin.

Some keepers ask whether it is necessary to scoop out the fecal mass, whether there might be a way for the mass to be broken down. It's possible with small insectivorous snakes and even with small rodent-eating snakes (usually less than 2 feet long) that feed on pinkies and fuzzy mice. It is not possible with larger snakes, such as adult boa constrictors, at least not in the relatively small enclosures we keep in our homes. In nature, the first step in fecal mass breakdown is usually performed by arthropods and other invertebrates, including fly maggots and other insect larvae, beetles, millipedes, snails, and worms. Many of these would prove undesirable in most people's homes, although this is an area that warrants further investigation.

Theoretically, using micro-organisms such as bacteria and fungi to compost snake feces should be possible given enough space and substrate. I have experimented by stirring the fecal mass of fish-eating snakes, including adult banded water snakes, in a large vivarium with 3 inches of substrate. From all appearances, including the smell test, the soft stools of these species are easily broken down.

Maintenance of BSS Substrates

How long can a BSS system remain viable? I have had BSS systems that housed lizards for more than two years without any addition or replacement of substrate. With snakes, I recommend partial replacement or addition of substrate every six months, because the BSS substrate tends to compact over time. Partial replacement of about 50 percent of the substrate also helps reduce accumulation of minerals, nitrates, and possibly certain pathogens in the substrate. On the other hand, I have three experimental setups that have successfully passed the one-year mark, including my original water snake setups. I did add 25 percent (by volume) additional substrate material to make up for compaction. The substrates are still functional and the enclosures are still odorless.

What About Disease?

There is a widespread belief that all bacteria are harmful and cause disease. What many people do not realize is that bacteria make the living world go round. For all forms of life, bacteria act as nanotechnological agents; they are

A plastic hand rake is a useful for mixing or stirring substrate.

miniature biological machines. Bacteria phobia is widespread in herpetoculture, a myth even spread by veterinarians, who are influenced by training that emphasizes pathogenic bacteria. In my experience, many veterinarians are obsessed with the sterility of reptile captive environments and phobic about substrate contamination. In fact, substrate contamination is a problem only when waste matter is not broken down by biological agents or surface fecal pathogens are not reduced by stirring them into deeper substrate levels. Once the substrate is bioactive, the dominant soil substrate bacterial populations compete with and overcome many other bacteria, including some of the GI tract/fecal pathogens that are of concern to keepers.

With the BSS system, it is important to stir bacteria-containing waste residue and secretions from the cloaca or mouth so that the microbes are mostly moved below the surface to an inhospitable environment. The small percentage remaining on the surface is distributed, so the surface pathogen density is low. A question that deserves investigation is what happens to the eggs and spores of reptile parasites in a bioactive system. Very likely, other bioactive agents such as soil nematodes, earthworms, and certain arthropods play a role in reducing the levels of these potential pathogens.

With this system, the primary food for vivaria bacteria comes from substrate components and waste residue produced by the animals we keep. As a result, the bacterial populations that proliferate in the substrate are those that are able to break down and utilize those particular nutrients. An ecological system, sometimes called the "soil food web," is formed. In this web, a variety of organisms compete for nutrients available in the substrate. The organisms range from viruses and bacteria to protozoa, nematodes, earthworms, and a wide range of arthropods, including harmless soil mites, spring tails, millipedes, centipedes, beetles, and others. Under vivarium conditions, we see competition that usually ends with the dominant bacterial populations that are best able to survive under the vivarium conditions and make use of the nutrient input.

One consequence is that other bacteria, including species potentially pathogenic to reptiles, are unable to compete and survive in a substrate with extensive bacterial colonization. Thus, a healthy bioactive substrate might have a probiotic effect against bacterial pathogens in vivaria.

As circumstantial evidence, most species of snakes I have tested burrow in or lie on the substrate when in shed; some species will even adjust their behaviors to the degree of substrate moisture, burrowing in the substrate for more moisture or perching on a rock or wood for less moisture. To date, I have not seen any signs of bacterial skin infections—even in species such as water snakes known to be prone to such infections when kept on moist substrates.

Snakes that were quarantined and treated for parasites prior to introduction to a BSS system environment have not shown signs of disease after seven months. Snakes that ingested small amounts of substrate in the course of feeding also have not shown signs of disease.

BSS and Commercial Operations

There are two types of commercial scale operations in herpetoculture—importers (where many animals are housed together in a single large enclosure) and breeders (where many animals are housed singly, in pairs, or in trios in relatively small, space-effective habitats). Each presents specific conditions and potential problems.

For importers, a significant cause of stress and disease in snakes is overcrowding. Creating topographical stratification, such as shelved shelter units, can play a significant role in reducing stress caused by the activity of other snakes and lack of shelters. Shelving can also help reduce exposure to fecal material accumulated on the enclosure floor. Ideally, importer setups should consist of rows of shelved shelters lining the sides of the enclosure and, if necessary, forming rows through the center of the enclosure, with large areas of open space in between. If regular and frequent replacement of the floor substrate is not possible, then a bioactive substrate stirred several times a week will prove beneficial and help reduce the spread of disease by contamination. One problem with using bioactive substrates in room-sized enclosures is that snakes often burrow into the substrate, making it difficult to locate and monitor individuals. The costs and benefits of BSS for importers warrant evaluation. I suspect that bioactive substrates will prove useful in large bin-type enclosures but not in room-sized, walk-in enclosures.

Breeder Setups

Many breeders use relatively small cage units to house snakes. If these units are well ventilated with screen tops and if they have water-holding bottoms, the bioactive substrate system can prove useful and reduce the labor of maintenance.

Whether this is practical or economical in such situations would have to be evaluated by individual breeders.

The BSS system is not appropriate for closed plastic storage boxes with perforated sides or covers, or for sliding storage-box shelf units. These systems fail to provide enough ventilation. As the water from the substrate evaporates it will produce a saturated relative humidity and condensation, favoring the growth of molds and bacteria that are detrimental to snakes. A second problem occurs when high numbers of aerobic bacteria produce dangerous levels of carbon dioxide because there is insufficient ventilation. The BSS system should never be used in systems with poor airflow. As an example, consider the Biosphere 2 closed-system experiment in Arizona that was halted because bacteria consumed too much oxygen, causing carbon dioxide to reach dangerous levels.

Multilayer Substrate Systems

If you have sufficient tank height and want to experiment with a multilayer bioactive substrate system, you can try to make the substrate more complex and even more effective.

With a triple-layer method, first place a drainage layer of fine gravel or hydroponic clay pellets (also sold as light expanded clay aggregate (LECA)) about 1-inch thick. Then, add a 2-inch layer of moistened peat moss mixed with 10-percent shredded green moss and 20-percent soil. Finally, top it with a 2- to 3-inch layer of bioactive substrate. The middle layer can be used as a vermile (earthworm containing) layer, which will improve biological processing and optimize beneficial bacterial loads. Add five earthworms (common earthworms, *Lumbricus terrestris*, are preferable to redworms or night crawlers) per square foot to the middle layer. The middle layer will also act as a source of retained moisture for the bottom of the bioactive layer, if needed.

Leaf Litter: In forest snake habitats, there is another substrate layer consisting of leaf litter. In vivaria, leaf litter is usually used only with species that require it or for specific display purposes, because litter creates a barrier to the passage of waste residues into the bioactive layer. The functions of leaf litter and the ways it benefits certain species, however, are worth considering. One of the most important effects of leaf litter is reducing the evaporative rate from the underlying substrate, so the soil right underneath the litter remains moist. Leaf litter also serves as an insulating layer that can help stabilize the temperature of an underlying bioactive layer. As a result of tannins, the pH under leaf litter is often acidic, which may inhibit bacterial growth. Typically, a fungal layer thrives under the leaf-litter layer. Leaf litter is also colonized by a wide range of organisms, many of which may play a role in the breakdown of wastes. Among the more interesting colonizers are those that feed on mites, such as predatory mites.

In vivaria, the use of leaf litter requires special maintenance procedures; it must be scooped aside to moisten and stir the bioactive substrate layer beneath. It also needs to be replaced regularly, as it will become unsightly. As a rule, leaf litter should only be used with species that are found on leaf litter in the wild. These species will commonly burrow in leaf litter to hide and when they are in shed.

Dried Moss: Live moss is difficult to keep in most vivaria and does best under conditions not always suitable for snakes. Although live moss is attractive in vivaria, it is a barrier for the passage of material from the ground surface into the substrate, so it is generally undesirable except in patches for decorative effect. Moistened dried green moss from nurseries or collected from forest or bog floors can be used to decorate portions of the vivarium surface and will even be used by some snakes as temporary moist resting areas. The moss should be replaced whenever it looks too ragged or if fouled. It can serve some of the functions of a leaf-litter layer.

Boosting Substrate Biological Activity

Various small organisms can be added to substrates to boost their activity. Among the best are earthworms, as long as your bottom soil layers are moist enough. Earthworms feed directly on the fecal residue of some snakes and process soil bacteria. You can try other arthropods, as well. For example, some species of beetle and millipedes will feed on fecal waste.

Substrate Pests

During the sequence of ecological changes that occurs in the substrate in the BSS system, a high level of fungal growth permeates the substrate, attracting fungus gnats, harmless psorid flies that unfortunately breed and multiply quickly. Fungal strands in the early stages of bioactivation of the substrate are normal. In one of my experiments I used cocoa husk mulch, which consistently generated extensive fungal growth and a proliferation of fungus gnats during the warmer months. The result can be an unsightly number of gnats that last up to eight weeks. By then, the stirring of fecal residue in the BSS substrate results in increasing bacterial levels, leading to a rapid decline in the fungal invasion. As this occurs, gnat numbers dwindle and eventually disappear.

Other pests may be introduced, usually with contaminated soils of purchased plants rather than bagged substrates. These include snails and slugs, which are easily removed, ants, small centipedes, and millipedes, which are not always easily removed. Ants are annoying to snakes and every effort must be made to prevent nest formation in a snake vivarium.

Substrate Design

The standard method of substrate design is to place a single even layer on the bottom of the vivarium. However, alternative designs provide certain advantages, particularly with ground-dwelling snakes.

The alternative to an even layer is an uneven one, with subtle hills and valleys. This should be done only in large vivaria, preferably with a perimeter three times or more the length of the snake. The most widely used substrate design is to create a raised area of substrate toward the

To water a vivarium from the bottom up, simply place a piece of pipe reaching just above the desired substrate height before adding the soil mix. By slowly pouring water in the pipe, the soil will moisten from the bottom up and reach the roots of plants without soaking the substrate surface.

back of the vivarium with a lower layer in the front. The deep layer in the back allows for introducing larger plants. One of the great advantages of a multilevel substrate is found when watering the substrate. By pouring the water in a depressed area, the moisture will spread from the ground up, watering the base of the plants, minimizing the need for excess water, and preventing the surface of the raised layers from getting wet. This effectively creates moisture zones in a vivarium.

Two variations best used in long tanks are what I call the "valley design" and the "T design." With the valley design, I create raised areas in the back and sides of a vivarium with a depressed valley running between them. When watering the substrate, water is poured in the valley and allowed to rise to half the substrate height of the raised areas. Placing an overhead light over one of the raised substrate areas also readily provides a warm gradient basking site. The T design has a raised back and a central raised bar that runs through the middle of the vivarium, from back to front. The raised center is perfect for designing a warm basking site using rocks or wood. It will keep background plants from being burned by an overhead spotlight.

CHAPTER 8:

LANDSCAPING

When keeping snakes, nothing is more important aesthetically and functionally than the landscaping of a snake vivarium. It is comparable to designing and furnishing a home—how you design it determines how its inhabitants behave.

At the onset, research and identify the kinds of landscape structures that are required and use this information to plan a particular design. The purpose of landscaping a vivarium is to structure the space inside—topographically and climatically—in a manner that meets the essential requirements of the species that lives in the vivarium, while also pleasing human observers.

By stratifying vivarium topography, you increase the surface areas that can be used for activity by a snake. With terrestrial snakes, for example, the simple introduction of a shelf with a surface area of 50 percent of the bottom of the enclosure increases the useful surface area by 50 percent. If the snake is arboreal, increasing the number of suitable perches will directly increase the surface available for activity. There are limits and parameters for doing this. If you overcrowd the inside of a vivarium with landscape structures you can create conditions that make any activity difficult, not unlike placing too much furniture in a room. There has to be a balance between three-dimensional structures and open space. This balance is learned through experience.

Topographical structuring of vivarium space also creates climatic zones. Shelves and shelters and their relationship to heat sources generate thermal gradients, strata that offer thermoregulatory choices important for the welfare of snakes. These same structures, depending on where they are placed, can also help create gradients of relative humidity.

A concrete shelter is integrated into the design of a desert vivarium

Finally, landscaping the vivarium, especially topographical structuring, will give it character and aesthetic impact.

Landscape Structures

Many snakes are active animals that will take advantage of the opportunities provided by landscape structures. The following are categories of landscape structures used by hobbyists when designing snake vivaria. As a word of caution, to prevent crush injuries securely anchor all landscape structures that could be displaced or toppled. Always test the stability of landscape structures before introducing snakes.

Terminology Related to Snake Habits

Diurnal: Active during the day

Nocturnal: Active at night

Crepuscular: Active around dawn or dusk

Terrestrial: Active at ground level

Arboreal: Active primarily in trees or shrubs

Semiarboreal: Spends part of the time in trees or shrubs

Fossorial: Burrows and is active in substrate

Aquatic: Active in water

Semiaquatic: Usually shoreline dwelling, sometimes active in water

61

Shelters

For a variety of reasons, most snakes limit their exposure to open areas and require some form of shelter. The confines of a shelter offer ecological and climatic conditions that are beneficial to snakes, allowing them to thermoregulate, conserve energy, reduce predation risks, and limit water loss. Just as with people, most snakes like the sense of security provided by the boundaries of walls and a ceiling, even if it is just for overnight. For snakes, the quality that provides this sense of security is not just the darkness within the shelter but, more importantly, the tactile sensation of being coiled in an enclosed space. When resting, many snakes like the security of feeling a high degree of surface contact between their own coiled bodies and the surfaces that define the shelter. Thus, a good shelter is an accessible enclosed space, large enough to contain a snake but small enough for the snake to feel a high level of contact from the surrounding surfaces.

As mentioned earlier, the insides of shelters encompass a different microclimate and microecology than open areas. The relative humidity in shelters is typically higher than in open air and temperatures are more moderate and subject to less fluctuation. During the peak midday heat, temperatures inside shelters are invariably cooler. For several hours at night they may be warmer, as rising heat from warmed soil becomes trapped within the shelter walls.

Cork over-lapped on wood or rock makes a natural-looking shelter.

Under this cork slab is a coiled California kingsnake. Relative humidity and substrate moisture are higher inside shelters placed on moist substrate.

Shelters protect snakes from wind chill and rain. In the wild, shelters can also harbor microfauna, such as pillbugs, millipedes, soil nematodes, predatory mites, earthworms, and centipedes, which serve as food for some snake species and also perform a sort of cleaning duty by eating mites.

For the above reasons, always provide a shelter for ground-dwelling and semiarboreal snakes. They are not usually required for burrowing snakes, such as sand boas or sunbeam snakes, which utilize the substrate as a shelter, nor with specialized arboreal snakes, which rest in the open. In vivaria, depending on the needs of a species and your design intentions, shelters can be created at different levels of the habitat using hollow cork sections, wood sections, hollow logs, securely stacked rocks, or commercially produced plastic, clay, or concrete shelters. For small arboreal or semiarboreal snakes, the spaces between the leaves of certain plants, such as larger bromeliads, can provide suitable shelters.

Shifting the position of its shelter can modify a snake's behavior. A standard herpetocultural approach has been to place shelters at ground level, with the result being that the snakes are invisible to the observer most of the time. However, variations in the design and position of shelters can raise snakes to a level that allows for better visibility.

63

The following are different kinds of shelters used by hobbyists for keeping various species of snake:

Ground-level shelters: These are the most widely used shelters, consisting of an inverted container with an access hole and placed on the substrate surface to accommodate ground-dwelling snakes. A variety of ground-level shelters for reptiles are now offered in the pet trade, ranging from molded-plastic hide boxes to faux-rock shelters made from plastic or concrete. Other types of ground-level shelters include hollow logs, cork bark sections, and clay huts. All of these are functional and some are attractive and natural looking enough to use with an artistic naturalistic vivarium.

A baby ball python gazes from under a cork bark shelter.

Another alternative for ground-level shelters is to stack cork bark sections, rocks, or broad sections of dried wood. Heavy materials such as rock or wood must be securely anchored together to prevent accidental crushing. For this reason, heavy stacked rock shelters are generally not recommended.

Open-front shelters: These are shelters with a large front opening. The large opening allows the viewer to observe the snake coiled in its shelter and the snake to look outward. They are generally not available commercially and

A Baja mountain kingsnake rests inside a clay shelter.

need to be custom made. Cork rounds placed on their sides with an enlarged lengthwise slit make attractive, natural-looking open-front shelters.

Arboreal shelters: These are shelters placed on shelves or posts, or attached to backgrounds—simulating an above-ground wood hollow. Arboreal and semiarboreal snakes use them and, if filled with a moist substrate, they may also be selected as egg-laying sites by these species. An easy way to create an arboreal shelter is to anchor a hollow cork log to a shelf. Another alternative is to use a wooden box, such as parrot egg-laying box, covered with cork bark to make it look natural. The box can be anchored to a shelf, tree branch, or the sides of an enclosure.

Lateral shelters: These are shelters without roofs that offer large areas of lateral contact against the sides of coiled snakes. They can be formed in the two-sided corners of tanks by adding an extra wall made of a rock, wood, or a plant. Adding vertical hollow logs, cork sections, rock, or wood, so that a three- or four-sided space is formed, can also form lateral shelters.

Overhead shelters: Many arboreal species will rest on a branch, positioning themselves beneath another branch or foliage, wood, or rock overhang that partially shades them.

In this vivarium a piece of cork was jammed between the wood perch and the side of the tank to create an above-ground shelter. This young Amazon tree boa readily adopted the shelter.

Some species will rest on the ground at the base of shrubs or other plants with foliage that hangs over them.

Underground shelters: These shelters are buried in substrate with access at the surface level. Although they are not common with hobbyists, the type designed with a window can have display appeal. Underground shelters can be carved from polyurethane foam or molded in plastic or concrete. If placed at the front of a tank, they can be lit from inside using a tiny incandescent bulb such as a Christmas tree light. They are particularly useful for displaying nocturnal snakes during the day.

This is a simple setup for a baby Colombian boa constrictor. In naturalistic setups, baby boa constrictors often perch above ground in the shelter of foliage.

Basking Sites

With most diurnal and crepuscular snakes, one or more basking sites should be incorporated into the vivarium design. A basking site provides a higher heat gradient than the rest of the vivarium, often accomplished by placing a spotlight over a heat-absorbing surface, such as rock or wood. For arboreal and semiarboreal species, basking sites consist of open areas of perches, preferably made of cork or dead wood. If bare branches of live plants are used as basking sites, be aware that long-term exposure will burn the leaves and wood, eventually killing the heated sections of plant.

Perches and Climbing Areas

Perches are above-ground activity and resting areas, usually made of wood or cork bark and accessible by ramps. They are required for semiarboreal and arboreal species, such as Amur rat snakes and emerald tree boas. If placed above water, they may also be used by some water snakes. The size and needs of a species determines the type of perches incorporated into a vivarium design. The diameter of a perch must allow for comfortable distribution of an animal's body weight. For most snakes, it ends up being between 50 and 100 percent of their midbody width.

Foliage overhanging a raised perching area provides security to arboreal species.

This is also the width of branches required by emerald tree boas and green tree pythons for perching. Semiarboreal species often prefer larger diameter branches for both climbing and coiling.

Wood branches are required as perches for semiarboreal snakes, like rat snakes, and with specialized arboreal species, such as tree boas and tree pythons. When selecting and positioning tree branches, remember that snakes that rest above ground require horizontal perching areas. Vertical or diagonal branches with a steep angle (more than 30 degrees) will not work. For tree pythons and boas, this means a smooth area of a single branch positioned horizontally above the ground. For arboreal perchers, like rat snakes, position a tree fork—approximately horizontally above ground. The fork will allow the snake to spread the weight of its coils over three or more contact points.

Semiarboreal species will also coil on broader tree limbs and cork slabs or rounds firmly anchored between the sides of a vivarium.

Biovine

This bendable manufactured material resembles a vine and can be coiled, dropped from a ceiling, or anchored rigidly across a vivarium to simulate vines in a tropical forest. It can also be used to create access ramps or even perching areas for small arboreal species. Live tropical vining and climbing plants can be trained to encircle or attach to the Biovine for an even more realistic vine effect. Biovine is best used with smaller snakes.

Cork Bark

Cork bark is the outer bark of the cork oak *(Quercus suber)* and is best known for its use in sealing bottles of wine. Usually imported from Portugal, cork is now available in its natural, unprocessed form from stores that specialize in reptiles. It is attractive and unbeatable for giving a vivarium character. Light and easily cut with a saw, it can be used to create backgrounds, ledges, shelves, and both vertical- and ground-level shelters. It is available in flat sections, rounds, or tubes, and as wall tiles. The rounded sections commonly sold as "cork tubes" or "cork round" can be broken up to make shelters or used whole to simulate vertical or fallen tree trunks. Flat pieces of cork can be used to create backgrounds, shelves, access ramps, or shelters (when rested on a rock or another piece of cork). Natural cork bark tiles are also available from companies that specialize in wall tiles. They are easy to install and make great vivarium backgrounds with insulating properties.

Hollow logs and tree trunk sections

In some tropical countries snakes often coil inside hollow logs or at the hollow base of trees during the day. In tropical forests, certain trees have a propensity to hollow out following injury. These hollow but still living trees form an extensive network of potential shelters and living areas for a wide range of animals. The insulating quality of the wood creates relatively stable microclimates and the hollow networks channel rising heat plumes. In captivity, large cork rounds are a good substitute for hollow logs because they are attractive, light, richly textured, and have insulating properties.

Problems with Wood

Pests: Often, commercially sold, dried, sand-blasted grape wood, as well as other woods that are pitted and hollowed, yield swarms of termites. Inspect woods carefully at the time of purchase for telltale signs of termite infestation such as fine wood-powder droppings.

Getting stuck: When wood branches are stacked to create perches, the areas where branches join can form narrow hollows that can trap the tip of a tail or even a small body. Luckily, this is an uncommon occurrence as little can be done to prevent it other than sealing the area of juncture with silicone or hot glue. The last incident I had was with a female Indonesian Pacific boa. I looked in the tank and couldn't figure out why she remained in the same stretched out position with her tail up between two stacked perching branches. After a few hours with no change, I decided to examine the situation and found that her tail was wedged between two branches.

Another possible source of problems are hollow logs with fissures and cracks large enough to allow a head to go through but not the midbody. Examine branches and hollow logs for possible risks and enlarge or seal any cracks you find.

Shelves

In vivaria, a shelf is simply a raised activity area constructed of wood, sections of cork bark, molded plastic, or concrete. Shelves serve several purposes. They increase functional surface area (akin to adding a second floor to the inside of a vivarium), serve as perches for semiarboreal species, and can create a thermal gradient if positioned under a heat light. In addition, they serve to anchor land-

Clay shelters and imitation rock shelters are readily available in the pet trade and can be integrated into the design of naturalistic setups.

scape structures and can be platforms for feeding and watering snakes. The minimum height for a tank to accommodate a shelf is usually at least one-half the length of the snake housed inside.

Access Ramps

Access ramps are landscape structures that allow snakes to easily reach shelves, raised branches, and shelters. They are usually made of wood branches or cork bark slabs diagonally positioned between the ground and the area to be accessed. To prevent injury, firmly anchor access ramps in place. If necessary, use silicone sealer, hot glue, or screws.

The Archeological Ruin Theme

An alternative to the naturalistic theme is to introduce human elements that suggest altered nature, commonly in the form of some type of ruin. Achieving this effect requires some thought and research, including finding appropriate materials to simulate a ruin. A common theme is the temple ruin, whether Mayan, Aztec, Greek, or Roman. To create this theme use simulated architecture of molded concrete or fiberglass to reproduce collapsed columns and integrate stone blocks and a variety of plants into the design. This type of setup must be large, often taking up a sizable portion of the room.

Another common theme is the "old stone wall." For this effect, use old bricks or stones arranged and anchored firmly in place to simulate a deteriorating wall overtaken by plants and vines. Snakes end up using hollows in the wall as shelters and the various blocks as climbing and basking areas.

CHAPTER 9:

PLANTS FOR SNAKES

One of the key elements that will transform a vivarium into a form of visual art is live plants. Plants bring color and interesting form to the composition and add three-dimensionality to the design. When planted in a bioactive substrate they play an intrinsic role in substrate ecology and the cycling of nutrients. They also provide shade and shelter. Arboreal and semiarboreal snakes use tree forms as both activity and resting areas. The proper selection and placement of plants is instrumental to achieving balance and design in the art of keeping snakes.

Most people have bad experiences keeping plants with snakes. Invariably, the plants are toppled and crushed, and end up drying out. Most authors of books on snake care recommend using plastic plants with snakes, but that simply changes keeping snakes like laboratory animals into kitsch (art in bad taste). Plastic or silk plants should always be a last resort. If used (and I mention this with great reluctance) every effort should be made to obtain high-quality fakes that are good enough to fool someone into thinking they are real. I have seen some interesting displays where high-quality artificial orchids were included among live plants and were real enough to fool you unless they were closely inspected.

There are three main reasons that live plants die in snake tanks: inappropriate plant species, lack of light and water, and overcrowding of plants. With the proper selection and attention to providing the right growing conditions, several kinds of live plants thrive in snake displays. There are many reasons for using live plants in snake enclosures. First, nothing conveys a feeling of nature and quality of design like live plants. The addition of live plants alone will immediately transform a sterile cage into a naturalistic vivarium. Also, live plants are key agents in turning your vivarium into a bio-system. The roots provide surface areas for bacterial growth, bind substrate, reduce water loss, and channel nutrient and water intake from the substrate. They also absorb waste by-products that can accumulate in the substrate, including ammonia and nitrates. In addition, as live plants grow they serve as changing landscape structures. As they are allowed to expand or to fill in they are a means of designing the topography of a vivarium. Through pruning and shaping, many plants in the confines of vivaria achieve an attractive bonsai form. Plants add beauty to the display and become a critical element of the aesthetics of the vivarium. If you want a quality snake display, use live plants.

Planting Vivaria

A baby albino banded water snake bred by author rests under a foliage overhang.

You must always remember that a vivarium differs from a terrarium in that its primary objective is the maintenance and display of live animals. Plants are not the central element in a vivarium—the animals are. The animals' activity and requirements direct the dynamics inside the vivarium walls. Always keep in mind the requirements of snakes as well as the following rules of plant use.

1. Plants should cover no more than a third of the ground surface area available to snakes. You need to have open areas to monitor snakes and make use of a bioactive

substrate. An exception is vivaria with arboreal snakes, which spend all their time above the ground, but even then you should leave at least 50 percent of the vivarium floor unplanted.

2. Small snake species allow for a greater selection of plants than large ones because they're lightweight and won't readily crush plants.

3. There are standard rules of design. Tall plants are usually planted toward the back of the tank so as not to block front viewing, although you may want to plant one or two tall plants in the middle ground to increase the three-dimensionality of your design. Ground covers are always placed toward the front.

4. With arboreal and semiarboreal snakes, there are two alternatives to plant placement. The most common is to place vertically growing plants toward the back of the enclosure. In front of or between the plants at a level halfway to two-thirds the height of the tank, anchor perching branches securely by stacking and gluing. Make sure to use branches of an appropriate diameter for the perching snake.

   The other alternative is to use plants with side branches thick enough to hold a perching snake. However, the size of the shrubs or trees required makes this impossible in the small enclosures kept in most homes. As a result, using live plants for perching areas is usually only done with small to medium semiarboreal and arboreal snakes, such as small tree boas, green tree pythons, and carpet pythons.

5. The branch diameter of plants used for climbing or perching should be at least 50 percent the diameter of the bodies of the snake species within the vivarium.

6. With all snakes, except those arboreal specialists that spend the majority of their time on branches above the ground, leave large, open, unplanted areas in between midground plants. Remember, most ground-dwelling snakes will not climb over shrubs and tall plants, but given the opportunity will go around and between them. The open areas also allow for easy maintenance, fecal scooping, and stirring of substrate.

7. Foreground plants and ground covers have limited uses, depending on the species kept. Medium to large ground-dwelling snakes will eventually crush foreground plants and ground covers. Ground covers often have shallow roots and require frequent watering, something that is not desirable with many snake species. Foreground plants can work with small semi-arboreal snakes and with arboreal species.

Change Plants as Snakes Grow

This baby western hognose snake, which was eventually raised to adulthood in a naturalistic setup, spent extended periods coiled in this aristocrat plant *(Haworthia fasciata)*.

As a rule, combining plants with pencil-thin baby snakes and small species is a no-brainer. Baby snakes are so light that they will not damage most houseplants, but that will change as the snakes grow larger. In nature, as snakes grow there is often a shift in their niche and activity areas. Thus, lizard-eating babies that once climbed herbaceous plants and shrubs now climb larger shrubs and trees and hunt baby birds. Keeping plants in a snake vivarium is easy with small to medium snakes, but the selection becomes limited as snakes grow larger and their weight and activity crush soft-leafed and thin-stemmed plants. With larger snakes, plants primarily serve decorative purposes in the background or middle ground of a vivarium, rather than as activity or perching areas.

Plant Adjustment

I wish I had some sure-fire formulas on plant use with snakes, but there are too many factors in the design of vivaria to make this possible. You will have to constantly fine-tune the design of your vivarium depending on a snake's growth and behaviors. It is a process of experimentation, removing plants and replacing them with more suitable species, hunting for new candidates, adjusting placement, and pruning and training plant growth. If you make it a point to regularly work on improving the design and look of your vivarium, you will eventually build a solid design foundation that you will be able to maintain. The process and final result are what make the art of keeping snakes so interesting. Learning which plants thrive with your snake species is a worthy challenge, as is finding that perfect equilibrium between filling the needs of a snake, creating a working vivarium system, and designing an artistic composition.

How to Introduce Plants

When growing plants hydroponically, in gravel and water or in LECA hydroponic pellets, wash the roots free of all soil prior to introduction into the growing medium.

There are two ways of growing plants in vivaria: introduce them in pots that are buried in substrate or plant them directly in the substrate. Each has advantages and flaws. The advantage of burying pots in the substrate is that plant growth and root spread can be controlled. Trees or shrubs with roots that will invade the substrate and compete with shallower rooted species for water and nutrients should be introduced in pots. The use of pots also allows for localized watering and fertilizing of plants. The negative aspect of growing plants in pots is that they are more prone to drying out if you forget to water them, and the roots cannot use the nutrient products of waste breakdown in a bioactive substrate. Plants that are set directly into substrate can do this, as well as provide areas for bacteria and other microfauna to grow or congregate through their root systems. As a rule, plant smaller plants with less extensive root ystems directly into substrates, but keep larger, faster-growing plants in pots. If you decide to keep a snake on a dry substrate, the only logical choice is to introduce plants in pots.

Feeding Plants

Use a liquid houseplant fertilizer solution (I use Miracle Gro) at a quarter the recommended strength every one or two months during the spring and summer to help promote the growth and health of vivarium plants. To do this, pour about a quarter cup of diluted fertilizer solution at the base of a plant and follow with an equal amount of water to drive it toward the roots.

Plant Selection

There are hundreds of plant species that can be used in snake vivaria, but most are not available through standard plant outlets, such as large nurseries and garden centers. Plant and snake combinations are like design recipes; it would require at least a chapter per species to describe specific plant and design formulas. For these reasons, the plant selection presented here emphasizes species that are, for the most part, available through standard plant outlets. If you are interested in experimenting with unusual exotic plants, track down specialty nurseries through your local phone book, horticultural magazines, or Internet sites. You may have to buy some plants out of state by mail order.

Plant selection for vivaria depends on research and is determined by the vivarium conditions, design intentions, and the species, size, and habits of the snakes maintained.

Some hobbyists strive to gear their plant selection by continent: the plants should at least come from the same continent as the snake species they are kept with. Other hobbyists try to be more specific and will endeavor to track down plants from the same country of origin as a particular species. The great majority, however, simply select any plant that will survive under the particular vivarium conditions and meet their design criteria. No matter what your approach to plant selection, attempt to match the general climatic requirements. With tropical forest snakes that require heat and humidity, select tropical plants. In vivaria displaying snakes from arid or rocky areas, sparsely plant with plant species that are tolerant of dry conditions and convey an arid-adapted feel.

The following is a selection of plants that are readily available, accompanied by information on their continent of origin, general climatic requirements, growth patterns, and use with certain snake species.

Definitions of Climatic Requirements

Tropical: The term, as used here, includes subtropical species. These are plants from warm and humid areas that require moderate to high light and daytime heat between 70 and 85° F. They also need a relative humidity of at least 50 percent and a moist, loamy substrate, except for epiphytes. Epiphytes (plants such as orchids that grow on other plants, using them as mechanical support) require a well-

drained, coarse substrate, such as orchid bark, lava rock, or tree fern fiber. Nighttime temperatures for these species can drop into the 60s F at night. They are good choices for a wide range of subtropical and tropical snakes and fare well with temperate species as long as they are not exposed to prolonged cool winter temperatures.

Arid: Arid plants require bright light, heat above 75° F, and a well-drained, coarse, sandy soil. This category includes cacti, succulents, many caudiciforms, and arid-adapted shrubs and trees. Arid plants are best used with snakes from arid areas, such as rosy boas, spotted pythons, desert kingsnakes, desert rat snakes, and diadem snakes.

Bromeliads (*Bromeliaceae* spp.)

Tropical; South America

Bromeliads are members of the pineapple family, characterized by a rosette of broad, straplike leaves. They are often lauded as great vivarium plants, but, in fact, often fare poorly because their requirements aren't met, including heat, light levels, and a well-drained soil mix. Their growth pattern also limits their uses. After flowering, a plant produces several offsets (vegetatively produced clones) and dies. This requires that the sizeable dead plant be removed from the vivarium and the offsets collected to prevent them from taking over the tank. In vivaria with herps, use spineless species to prevent injury to the animals.

Some good bromeliad candidates are members of the genera *Neoregelia*, *Guzmania*, *Billbergia*, and *Vriesia*. They are best introduced in pots with an airy, well-drained soil mix that contains either orchid bark or crushed lava rock (perlite). The drainage material prevents base rot, which is common when these plants are overwatered. Introducing them in pots also allows you to easily remove them when they require maintenance and facilitates the removal of a dead mother plant or excess offsets. Bromeliads can also be grown in epiphytic logs and in epiphyte backgrounds. Because most of the species are epiphytes from humid forests, they are best used with semiarboreal and arboreal tropical forest species. Unfortunately, the dense overlapping leaves provide plenty of areas for snakes to conceal themselves, so for best viewing, use them in limited numbers.

Cacti (*Cactaceae* spp.)

Arid, tropical; the Americas

Keepers often wonder what cacti can be used with desert snakes. Most desert cacti require too much light to fare well in vivaria and the spines on many species can cause injury to both animals and owners. There is only one species of padded cactus that I have found works well in desert-type setups; that is the spineless opuntia tree *(Consolea falcata)*, available sporadically through standard nursery outlets.

For tropical snakes, there are several kinds of spineless epiphytic cacti (for example, epiphyllums and rhipsalis) that can be incorporated in setups and—depending on the design and conditions—can work well. Epiphytic cacti require well-drained soil, humidity, and good ventilation. Some can be trained to climb and grow on cork bark logs and backgrounds.

Except for tropical cacti, most cacti fare well under the lower relative humidity requirements of desert vivaria. Tropical cacti must have at least 60 percent humidity, while desert cacti require humidity below 60 percent.

The tree opuntia *(Consolea falcata)* has insignificant spines and is ideal for those wanting a cactus-type plant in their vivarium. Bright light is required.

Caudexed Plectranthus *(Plectranthus ernstii)*

Arid and tropical; Africa

This member of the Coleus family adapts to a variety of conditions and has felted, scented, semisucculent leaves. The base stems eventually swell and form a type of caudex. With some pruning, these plants end up looking like a short bonsai shrub. They also readily produce their stalks of bright blue flowers under lights. The stems are brittle and easily broken, but they work well with baby snakes and smaller, ground-dwelling snakes from drier areas, such as western hognoses. They'll also grow in tropical vivaria as long as the substrate has good drainage.

Chinese Evergreens (*Aglaonema* spp.)

Tropical; Asia

Aglaonema are ornamental aroids (members of the family Araceane) with relatively broad, soft leaves that are easily damaged by climbing snakes. Aglaonema have a limited use in snake vivaria—mostly with smaller terrestrial and semiaquatic species, although they can work with small, forest-dwelling snakes. Snake species with which they're recommended include garter snakes, water snakes, rough green snakes, viper boas, Indonesian dwarf Pacific boas, baby tree boas, and green tree pythons. When used with baby arboreal or semiarboreal species, there is usually a point that the plants incur significant damage, mostly

Chinese evergreens *(Aglaonema)* are used to landscape a setup for a baby Andesian milk snake.

crushed leaves. When this occurs, replace them with a tougher species.

Croton *(Codiaeum variegatum pictum)*
Tropical; Asia

I've only recently experimented with this species. Given enough heat, light, and humidity, the narrow-leafed forms fare reasonably well in vivaria. The leaves are leathery; in time, with regular pruning, the stems will become thick enough to bear the weight of smaller snakes. A flaw is that croton forms an extensive binding root system in the substrate, so introduce it in a pot.

Dragon Trees (*Dracaena* spp.)
Tropical; Africa, Asia

Dracaenas grow as canes topped with rosettes of straplike leaves. They are medium thick and usually tough enough to accommodate most medium-sized snakes, but not able to cope with repeated crushing by large snakes. Still, they are overall good performers. They make good midground plants when young, and good background plants when they develop tall canes. Smaller arboreal snakes may choose to coil and rest between their broad leaves. Larger snakes will use them as access ramps.

The most resistant to snake activity is the widely available *Dracaena deremensis* and its many cultivars. *D.*

Dracaenas are generally good choices with tropical snakes. With larger species, such as emerald tree boas, use them as backgrounds. Smaller snakes will find shelter between their leaves.

deremensis compacta, with its dense rosettes of thick, dark green leaves is well suited as a midground plant when small and as a background plant after it grows taller. The popular cornstalk plant *(D. fragrans massangeana)* and ribbon plant *(D. sanderiana)* do reasonably well when small with smaller species of snakes. In time, however, these two species grow too large and their soft leaves are easily crushed by larger snake species.

Related Species:
Song of India *(Pleomele reflexa)*
is a variegated Asian plant that looks like a dense-growing dracaena. Leathery, variegated leaves cover its stalks and form a dense rosette. It has a smaller leaf-spread than dracaenas and does well in vivaria.

Star of India *(Pleomele reflexa variegata)* has sturdy leaves that spiral up the stem. It performs extremely well in tropical snake vivaria housing small to medium snakes.

Dwarf Umbrella Trees (*Brassaia arboricola* and cultivars)
Tropical; Australia, Asia
These members of the Aralia family are very adaptable and trainable in vivaria. Dwarf umbrella trees are characterized by crowns of compound leaves, with leaflets forming a round umbrella. The leaves tend to cluster around the growing tips of the branches while the trunk and branches are bare. Dwarf umbrella trees typically grow vertically, so they are ideal as background plants. The stems can also be bent to form horizontal perching and climbing areas. Their

A baby boa constrictor is coiled in a dwarf umbrella plant *(Schefflera arboricola).*

flaws include fast growth and the need for regular pruning in order to prevent screen-cover clustering. Use them with tropical arboreal and semiarboreal species.

Other Araliads:
Another member of the Aralia family, the Balfour aralia *(Polyscias balfouriana)*, has relatively thick, rounded leaves and will work with small to medium arboreal species. It is sporadically available through standard nursery outlets.

Variegated Balfour aralia is a good background plant in tropical vivaria. They work well with a variety of smaller arboreal snakes but the thin stems will bend or snap if climbed on by larger animals.

Elephant Bush *(Portulacaria afra)*
Arid and tropical; Africa
This is a neat bush that resembles a jade plant but has smaller, more rounded leaves. Its requirements are the same as for jade plants. In time, it develops attractive proportions, a thick trunk, and branches with small succulent leaves. With a little pruning, it can be made to look like a bonsai tree. The variegated green and pale yellow form is readily available and is said to tolerate lower light conditions than the typical form. I've used them with small to medium snake species from drier areas, such as diadem snakes, mountain kingsnakes, and western hognose snakes.

Ferns *(Nephrolepis* spp.)
Temperate, tropical; Global
Most ferns will not survive in snake vivaria; they can't withstand the activity and crushing. Among the few ferns that can fare well are members of the genus *Nephrolepis*, including the Boston and lace ferns *(Nephrolepis exaltata)* and their many cultivars, and the pigmy sword fern *(N. duffii)*.

The only problem with *Nephrolepis* in vivaria is that they often fare too well and become invasive monsters, sending out runners and eventually overtaking the display. I've used them on the bottom of tanks with tropical, arboreal specialists, such as green tree pythons, carpet pythons, and tree boas. They also work as background plants with smaller temperate and tropical ground dwellers, as long as you keep them controlled by clipping and removing the ever-invasive offsets.

Among my favorite ferns, and one that will work reasonably well with tropical species, is the birds nest fern *(Asplenium nidus* and cultivars), which grows large but relatively slowly. Birds nest ferns like a moist, airy, well-drained substrate and moderate heat. Keeping your birds nest fern too moist will rot its base and cause it to die.

There are several other thick-leaved ferns, such as the *Aglaomorpha*, that can work with snakes, but most tend to grow too large and only prove useful in roomy setups. If you want to experiment with other ferns, consider three criteria: thick leaves, tolerance of warm temperatures, and the ability to survive at moderate humidity levels.

Haworthia (*Haworthia* spp.)
Arid; Africa

These are small, rosette-forming succulents in the lily family. Most are too small to be useful with snakes, but the larger species and cultivars are worth considering with smaller desert snakes. The most readily available species, the aristocrat plant *(Haworthia fasciata)*, is hardy, decorative, and suitable for vivaria housing snakes, such as western hognose, Egyptian diadem snakes, and small kingsnakes.

Hoyas (*Hoya* spp.)
Tropical; Australia, Asia

These members of the milkweed family (Asclepiadaceae) are tough, thick, and relatively slow-growing climbing vines. They are good choices for small to medium arboreal or semiarboreal snakes.

In terms of selection, tropical species such as silver pink vine *(Hoya purpureo-fusca)* are better suited for snake vivaria than subtropical species such as the standard green wax plant *(H. carnosa)*, which prefers cooler (low 70s F) room temperatures. The variegated wax plant and the Hindu rope (*H. carnosa*, variegata, and *H. carnosa*, compacta) are cultivars that are more heat tolerant than the standard form and fare well in vivaria. All species do best in well-drained soil, with moderate to bright light and airy conditions. Smaller species, such *H. bella*, can be grown and raised in epiphytic logs, with the vines allowed to drop for a curtained effect. In the winter, growth slows to a standstill, but in spring and summer, hoyas send out runners that eventually climb branches and logs and spread on the ground surface. They are best planted at the base of wood, such as stumps and branches. The weight of large, heavy snakes may snap off leaves at the base. Hoyas are sensitive to overly moist conditions and do best with some drying out between watering, as well as good drainage in the substrate. Besides the handful of species that have become standard fare in the nursery trade, a large number of other species are available through mail-order specialty nurseries.

Jade Plant *(Crassula argentea)*
Arid; Africa
Grown in a sandy substrate with good light and heat, jade plants perform well with snakes from dry areas. Their shapely shrublike appearance, thick trunk, and elegant leaves can help offset the lanky appearance of some of the other popular desert vivarium species, such as sansevieria and pony-tailed palms. The main reasons jade plants fare poorly as vivarium plants are overwatering, which rots the base, and poor light, which results in thin, weak, and stretched growth.

The pony-tailed palm *(Beaucarnea recurvata)* performs well with desert snakes.

Palms (*Chamaedora* spp.)
Tropical and arid; Global
When small, several kinds of palms make nice background plants for various tropical snakes. The problem is that most grow too large and cannot be pruned. For anything less than room-sized vivaria, the only readily available species that can be used short term are young parlor palms and bamboo palms (*Chamaedora elegans* and *C. erumpens*). Another worthwhile dwarf palm for larger vivaria, but one not always available, is the dwarf fish-tail palm *(C. metallica)*.

Philodendrons (*Philodendron* spp.)

Tropical; South America

Several of these popular aroids have large leaves and trunks or stems. Many grow large, so they will only work in larger vivaria. One of the best species for shoreline or tropical vivaria is philodendron Xanadu. It looks exotic and will grow in soil or hydroponically in moist gravel or water. In larger setups, small and medium snakes will use the stems of larger philodendrons and the related monstera as climbing ramps. Some will hide in the crown; others may even stretch or coil on leaves. Refer to a horticultural reference, such as the book *Tropica* (1992) to learn about the different types of philodendrons and their growth patterns.

The cut leaves of philodendron Xanadu make it a very attractive addition to larger tropical or shoreline displays. It can grow between 15 and 30 inches, depending on the conditions. Keep it small by growing it in small pots that restrict root spread.

Pony-Tailed Palms *(Beaucarnea recurvata)*

Arid; North America

These attractive plants form a large caudex, topped with a crown of narrow, straplike leaves. They hail from arid areas of Mexico and rank as one of the hardiest houseplants. In large vivaria with good lighting, they will thrive and are ideal with snakes from open, dry areas, such as rosy boas, diadem snakes, and western hognose snakes. They are best used as background plants, although a single plant in the midground of a large setup will be effective for giving a three-dimensional look to the design.

What's a Caudex?

A caudex is a thick, swollen water-storage organ developed by a wide range of plant species, mostly to survive through extended periods of drought. Plants that develop a caudex are known in horticulture as caudiciforms. A caudex can be as small as a pea or as large as a Volkswagen and weigh several hundred pounds, depending on the type of species and its age. Caudexes often have great character, from the tortoise shell pattern of elephant foot plants *(Dioscoraea elephantipes)* to the green streaked bombax *(Bombax ellipticum)* and papery bark trunks of Burseras. The best-known caudiciforms are pony-tailed palms and those plants commercially sold as Madagascar palms *(Pachypodium lamerei).*

Pothos *(Epipremnum aureum)*
Tropical; Asia

This popular climbing vine is the weed of vivarium plants. It can be grown in low light or bright light, in soil or hydroponically, as long as the leaves are exposed to air. It's a good creeper and in tropical setups can be trained as a liana (a woody tropical vine forming natural ropes between branches) or to climb and cover wood and backgrounds. It's generally too weak to hold up to a snake's activities, but it's a good decorative plant. I've used it on the floor of arboreal setups containing green tree pythons and red-tailed rat snakes. Pothos also thrives in vivaria with smaller snakes and in shoreline vivaria (vivaria that simulate a water and land interface, such as the shoreline of a pond or stream). Try it with water snakes, garter snakes, and rough green snakes.

Snake Plants (*Sansevieria* spp.)
Arid and tropical; Africa

These tough, thick-leaved succulent members of the Liliaceae family consistently rank among the best vivarium plants. Most grow to 2 feet or more, so they are best used as background plants with ground-dwelling species. The most readily available are the various cultivars of *Sansevieria trifasciata*, sold through most nurseries, including the short, rosette-forming birds nest sansevieria

(S. trifasciata hahnii), which are short enough to use as midground plants.

Snake plants require well-drained soil (add bark or pumice) and a moderate amount of light. In desert vivaria, thick-leaved and cylindrical-leaved snake plants, if used sparingly, can add great character to a mostly bare display. Several of the cylindrical-leaved species have hard pointed tips that are best clipped off to prevent injury. All sansevieria require a well-drained substrate and moderate light (equal to bright, indirect sunlight) to fare well.

A rosy boa emerges next to a *Sansevieria kirkii pulchra.*

Weeping Figs (*Ficus benjamina* and cultivars)
Tropical; Asia

This is the mainstay shrub and tree of herpetoculture. Weeping figs are readily available and adaptable to a wide range of conditions. The leaves are not too large and their growth can be controlled. The flaws of *Ficus benjamina* are that they, like other ficus, exude latex when injured (leaves or branches are broken) and they drop leaves when environmental conditions change. The plant will die if kept too dry (the roots will desiccate) and if kept too wet (the roots will rot). That said, there are many patented cultivars and hybrids of weeping figs that are tougher and less prone to leaf drop, such as the series sold under the name Ficus of the Future. This series includes varieties with dark leaves, such as Ficus Indigo and Ficus Midnight, as well as small leaved varieties with compact growth, such as Ficus Rianne. Because the root systems of fig trees can invade the substrate and the growth can be rapid, control the growth and spread of these species by introducing them in pots and regularly pruning and shaping.

Other Fig Trees (*Ficus* spp.):
Tropical and arid; Global
Some specialty nurseries carry other ficus, including the Chinese banyan *(Ficus retusa nitida)* and small cultivars of the rubber plant *(F. indica)*. For drier, desert vivaria, the Mexican caudexed figs *(F. petiolaris* and *F. palmeri)* are excellent and can be trained into shapely, squat bonsai. *F. petiolaris,* with its large leaves veined in bright red, has become increasingly popular and is now occasionally available through large chain stores.

Figs number around 600 species, come in a variety of forms and growth patterns, and offer a great selection for vivarium landscaping. Many species are available through specialty nurseries. A little gem is the mistletoe fig *(F. diversifolia)* with its rounded triangular leaves and mistletoe-like fruit. Other species worth considering are the green island fig *(F. macrocarpa)* and the willow-leaf fig *(F. nerifolia).* Good lighting, warm temperature, and a moist substrate will allow many tropical figs to survive in vivaria.

Zamiaculcas *(Zamiaculcas zamiifolia)*
Arid and tropical; Africa
This succulent member of the philodendron family is one of the great houseplants. It is now grown commercially on a large scale. The vertical leaf stems are thick, succulent, and lined with rows of shiny leathery leaflets. Because it grows to about 2 feet high, it is best suited for taller vivaria.

It likes moderate not bright light and well-drained soil, and thrives with infrequent watering. As a background plant, it's a good choice for small to medium tropical snakes. If it grows too large for your setup, transfer it to a nice pot and use it as a hardy and elegant decorative houseplant.

Pony-Tailed Palm *(Beaucarnea recurvata)*

Tufts of straplike leaves grow out of a round caudex.

Calibanus hookeri is a caudiciform that performs well in desert vivaria but only with heat and bright lights. It can be bought from specialty succulent nurseries.

Calibanus hookeri

Tufts of tough, grasslike leaves grow out of a ball-like caudex that, over several years, can reach a couple of feet in diameter. I've successfully grown this plant under lights for many years, so it has passed my vivarium plant test. However, it does like strong light and heat during the summer months.

Elephant Bush *(Portulacaria afra)*

This is a neat shrub with a natural bonsai form. It performs well in warm desert vivaria even if illuminated only by an incandescent bulb focused on a basking site.

Jade Plant *(Crassula argentea)*

Jade plant can also fare well, but likes good light or it will become lanky and weak stemmed.

Ficus *(Ficus petiolaris)* and *(Ficus palmeri)*

These caudexed figs also grow in desert vivaria and can be trained to look like bonsai.

This desert vivarium interior boasts snake plants *(Sansevieria)* and other species suitable for keeping with smaller desert snakes, such as diadem snakes and rosy boas.

Snake Plants (*Sansevieria* spp.)

Snake plants are generally good performers in vivaria. Cylindrical and semicylindrical forms are better suited for desert vivaria. Clip off the pointed leaf tips of some species to prevent possible injury.

Xerosicyos dangii

This succulent slow-growing member of the cucumber family has tough stems and thick, round, disklike leaves. It is originally from Madagascar.

CHAPTER 10:

HEATING AND LIGHTING

Although many reptile breeders keep snakes in dark enclosures year round, observing snakes perform a range of natural behaviors depends on providing a natural day and night cycle. Lighting also allows plants to grow and shows off the design of the vivarium. Snakes must be provided with one or more heat sources so that they can self-regulate their body temperature.

Heating

All reptiles are ectotherms, meaning they regulate their body temperature through behavioral relationships with their environment. Many reptiles can raise their body temperatures 10° F or more above air temperature by

The Baja mountain kingsnake *(Lampropeltis zonata agalma)* is only bred by a few specialists but has great qualities as a display snake. Unlike most tricolor kingsnakes, the Baja mountain kingsnake often comes out during the day to bask.

absorbing heat from sunlight and radiant heat from rocks and the ground. No single factor is more important to a snake's health than providing a heat gradient that allows it to self-regulate its body temperature.

Ambient Temperature and Subtank Heating

With the LAM method of keeping snakes, a heat gradient/basking site is effectively and economically generated by a subtank heating unit, such as heat tape. However, this method cannot be applied to the BSS system, or naturalistic vivaria in general, because the substrate may dry and overheat. Drying or overheating the substrate will kill beneficial bacteria and plants.

With the BSS system, subtank heating pads, heat tape, or soil heating cables are connected to rheostats or thermostats and placed beneath enclosures to generate an even, ambient substrate temperature—in the low temperature range suitable for a species. Even soil heat generates a mild ambient air temperature, increases plant growth, and is appropriate for soil bacterial growth. Subtank heating that raises the soil temperature to 74–78° F is recommended for tropical species, but may not be necessary for maintaining most temperate species if their setups are kept at comfortable room temperatures.

Thermal Gradients and Basking Sites

In nature, the thermal gradients used by ectothermic animals are generated by solar radiation. Heat from the sun is absorbed, dissipated, stored, or reflected. It is the relationship with a particular heat mosaic, the pattern of different thermal gradients in an environment, that allows an ectotherm to regulate its body temperature within desirable operational limits. Initial heating of the environment is from above, so with most diurnal species you should try to reproduce that in your display vivaria.

Provide heat primarily with overhead incandescent lighting placed above basking sites of wood or rock that can absorb heat. The most common method is to place a reflector-type fixture with an incandescent bulb or spotlight on the enclosure's screen top and position it over the basking site. The unlit areas and shelters provide accessible cooler gradients, which will be sought by a snake if the temperature gets too high. Heat from an overhead source may—depending on the distance from the basking site and the moisture content of the substrate—also reach the ground level and warm the surrounding substrate. A moist substrate will effectively absorb overhead heat and spread it through the substrate layer. In enclosures less than 48 inches long, provide only a single basking site to ensure that a cool gradient can be maintained. You can provide an additional basking site for enclosures 48 inches or larger, as long as you check different areas of the vivarium with a thermometer to ensure you have the desired heat gradient.

With tall enclosures, place basking lights over branches or shelves to create a vertical temperature gradient. The upper structures close to the basking light will be warmer than ground-level sites.

Thermoregulatory Patterns

In nature, heat is not an on-and-off process but a pattern of onset and offset related to the sun. Typically, nights are cool. After the sun rises, the temperature gradually increases, peaking in the midday and early afternoon hours and then gradually cooling off as the sun sets. For several hours in the early evening, heat that was absorbed by rocks and ground is radiated, so the ground is warmer than the air.

Snakes adjust their behavior to these thermal patterns, often emerging in the morning to bask then retiring in shelters when ambient temperatures exceed optimal operating body temperature. Often, they re-emerge late in the day to take advantage of rock surfaces that have absorbed and retained heat into the evening hours. As a general rule, reptiles warm up rapidly and cool off relatively slowly. In vivaria, similar behavior patterns can be observed in relation to illuminated basking sites—snakes emerge from shelters in the morning to warm up, retire at midday, and reappear toward the end of the day.

Heating Nocturnal Snakes

Several species of snakes are nocturnal and only emerge at night. Nocturnal snake vivaria should be heated to normal levels during the day because, even if hidden, snakes may select shelters that receive diurnal heat. Increased daytime ambient temperatures will also raise their body temperature, allowing them to digest a meal ingested the previous night. Nocturnal snakes also benefit from nighttime heat gradients, including red incandescent or ceramic infrared heat lamps placed above basking areas.

Design a Thermal Mosaic

By designing areas of raised substrate and perching sites and by positioning lights over basking sites, you can create three or more thermal zones in a vivarium. Varying the temperature or placement of these zones shapes a snake's behavior and allows for interesting experiments related to thermoregulation. With the art of keeping snakes, however, we try to stick with certain principles—lower elevations within the vivarium are kept cooler and some areas at ground level or at a raised basking site are kept warmer. Heated areas should be within the range desirable for a particular species.

General Lighting

For general display purposes and for growing live plants, illuminate the length of the vivarium with two or more fluorescent bulbs. It is best to use full-spectrum bulbs, because they provide an attractive light quality for viewing. To prevent a high level of flickering and to extend bulb lives, avoid cheap magnetic ballast shop-light fixtures and use the more expensive fluorescent fixtures with electronic ballasts.

Compact fluorescent fixtures and bulbs are an alternative and increasingly popular method for providing inexpensive lighting for plants and general illumination. They are now readily available in long tube forms in the aquarium trade. Short tube forms and coiled types of compact fluorescent lighting can be found in large chain hardware stores.

Some species of snakes may benefit from UV-A (ultraviolet-A) and UV-B (ultraviolet-B) from sources such as sunlight or reptile UV-B bulbs, but no definitive research has been done in this area.

Sunlight and reptile UV-B bulbs are recommended for some herps because UV-B radiation likely participates in the synthesis of vitamin D_3 (required for the absorption of calcium and other metabolic functions). Thus, a source of UV-B may be important for many herbivorous and insectivorous reptiles that do not have access to a dietary source of D_3. This does not apply to most of the snakes kept in captivity, however, because they feed on whole vertebrate prey with livers rich in vitamin D_3. The theory that vertebrate-eating snakes do not require a UV-source for D_3 synthesis is supported by the success of commercial breeders, who have achieved great longevity and fecundity in snakes (in all commercially bred species) maintained with no UV exposure.

Some diurnal species that feed on insects and other invertebrates such as rough green snakes might derive benefits from UV-B exposure. In addition, there may be secondary benefits from exposure to UV-A and UV-B sources for vertebrate-eating snakes in captivity. Besides possible psychological benefits, some speculate that UV-B exposure has a bactericidal effect on the skin of snakes that bask. The possible benefits of UV exposure deserve further investigation, but it is safe to say UV-B is not a requirement for most of the snakes offered in the hobby and general pet trade. If interested in experimenting with UV sources, consider replacing a standard fluorescent bulb with a reptile UV-B bulb.

Photoperiod

The term "photoperiod" refers to the amount of time per day that an organism is exposed to light. In nature, organisms living near the equator are exposed to about twelve hours a day of sunlight year round. Organisms living in subtropical and temperate zones have winters with short days and long nights and summers with long days and short nights. Little methodical research has been done on the role of photoperiod in snakes. Many commercial breeders keep their snakes under mostly dark or dim conditions year-round without any effort to control light exposure and consistently get good results keeping and breeding different species. One view is that most snakes avoid light most of the day so it is unlikely that photoperiod is a significant factor in regulating their behaviors. Nonetheless, several commercial breeders and hobbyists strive to control photoperiod, usually by reducing the number of hours of light exposure to ten hours a day during the winter months and increasing light exposure to fourteen hours a day during the spring and summer months. Snakes that are diurnal and active during the day may be more influenced by photoperiod than other snakes, a possibility that deserves further investigation. In indoor vivaria, the photoperiod is easily controlled by connecting lights to an electrical timer.

The Mysterious Nightlife

Part of snakes' mystery is what they do when we cannot see them; for many species this means nightlife. As many snake collectors know, one of the best ways to find snakes is to go out at night in a car and search roads running through natural habitats. Often, snakes lie on warm asphalt roads after sunset. In a tropical forest, walking on trails with a powerful flashlight at night usually reveals a number of snakes prowling about. The fact is, when people retire for the night, many snakes come out and play. In captivity, it is possible to design vivaria that open a unique window on the life of snakes and allow us to observe their nocturnal activities.

To observe nightlife, shut off bright lights and turn on either low-wattage red incandescent bulbs (such as used in many zoo night displays) or dark blue lights, called "moonlights" or "nightlights" in the pet trade. In my personal experience, 25-watt red incandescent bulbs are a better choice for observing nocturnal reptile and amphibian species than moonlights. Specialized hobbyists interested in night behaviors have designed systems where nightlights on timers come on for a few hours after the standard lights go off. This allows them to observe their snakes at night but provides a very different aesthetic experience. The color of the lighting gives the display a unique spectral quality, as does the reflection of snake scales and eyes: you have the sense of peering into a secret world inhabited by ghostly forms. Experimentation will allow you to determine if the species you are keeping respond better (meaning they appear to be more active and display higher levels of exploratory behavior) to red lights or to moonlights. Nocturnal lighting systems can make the ownership of night-owl species a rewarding adventure.

Preventing Fires

The use of electrical heating and lighting devices present potential fire risks and you should take great care to make sure they are not placed near flammable materials.

There are various ways that heat lamps can cause fires. Never place them near flammable materials such as curtains. Make sure light fixtures are securely anchored; they can be toppled by free-roaming pets or children, and can ignite rugs, clothing, slipcovers, and dog beds. Select a ceramic-base spotlight fixture capable of handling the wattage bulb you intend to use. A fixture may overheat and burn if it is not appropriate for the wattage or the type of bulb used. When removing an incandescent light from the top of a tank during maintenance, always turn it off and put it back in its original position after you're done. Fires and burn damage often occur when a keeper removes a fixture set on a timer and places it on a table or the floor, forgetting to return it after completing the task. When the timer turns the light on, the bulb burns whatever it is on.

Additional fire risks are linked to the use of subtank heating pads, although not usually when used with naturalistic vivaria. The classic case occurs when a subtank heating pad is used without being connected to a rheostat. The heating pad is placed beneath a glass tank containing wood shavings that is kept on a wooden table. Heat builds up under the tank, cracks the glass bottom, and ignites the shavings. To prevent this, connect the subtank heating pad to a rheostat or, preferably, a thermostat. Also, raise the bottom of the enclosure to allow cool air flow beneath it, preventing heat build up. In naturalistic vivaria containing soil, which is not readily flammable, the risks of fire from a cracked tank bottom are low.

In addition to the above precautions, always install a smoke or fire alarm in rooms with reptile enclosures warmed by electrical heating devices. If pet snakes are kept in a child's bedroom, review escape plans periodically.

CHAPTER 11:

RELATIVE HUMIDITY

Relative humidity is the measurement of the amount of water vapor contained in the air at a given temperature. It is expressed as a percentage relative to the potential water storing capacity of air at that given temperature. For example, 70 percent relative humidity and 80° F means that, at the temperature indicated, the air contains 70 percent of the amount water vapor it could store. Air humidity is measured with an instrument called a hygrometer.

Relative humidity is important for many reptiles and influences evaporative water loss and shedding in snakes. Most snakes spend extended periods of time inside shelters, where relative humidity tends to be higher than in open air. In captivity, most snakes easily compensate for water loss by drinking, but some tropical and burrowing species require high relative humidity (70 to 90 percent) to fare well.

Humidity Gradients

One effect of heating a tank, whether from below or from above, is an increase in the rate at which water evaporates. The initially increased relative humidity decreases and the vivarium eventually dries out. You must regularly add water to the substrate to help maintain moderate humidity levels in vivaria. In addition, trapping water vapor creates high relative humidity gradients in vivaria. When heated, water tends to rise and dissipate as water vapor unless trapped. In captivity and in the wild, shelters trap water vapor and have a higher relative humidity than open areas.

Sheltered areas, whether formed by plants or rock ledges, also trap water vapor. In vivaria with shelters, plant shade, and leaf litter, the behavior of snakes shifts in relation to these moisture gradients. Green tree pythons, for example, often descend and coil in a moist tree hollow or on the ground at the base of plants when in shed.

Increasing Relative Humidity

With arboreal snakes that don't use shelters, regular misting once or twice a day to generate water vapor increases relative humidity levels inside the vivarium. Another way to increase relative humidity is to partially cover the screen top of the tank. A hygrometer allows you to measure the air humidity. For snakes that use shelters, increase relative humidity in the shelter by daily misting inside or placing the shelter over a shallow container containing a moist substrate such as sand. As the water evaporates from the container, the humidity increases inside the shelter.

Ventilation

Snakes do not fare well under conditions of high humidity with poor ventilation, which is why screen tops are best for most snake species. With the BSS method there is also the risk of excess CO_2 buildup in poorly ventilated systems. Evaporated water from the substrate and water container goes through day/night condensation cycles that can promote high levels of surface bacterial and fungal growth. Use enclosures with screen tops or sides.

Environmental Monitoring and Control

Certain environmental monitoring tools are required for keeping snakes. One tool is a thermometer, ideally one that is electronic and digital with external probes that can be placed in different areas of the tank. Many hobbyists simply use the inexpensive stick-on strip thermometers currently sold in the reptile trade and place them in an area that gives them a general temperature reading. Another useful tool, but not a requirement with many snake species, is a hygrometer. Inexpensive, but not very accurate, humidity gauges are available in the reptile trade, including combos sold with stick-on thermometers. Light meters, which are used to measure the light received by plants, are also useful.

The only widely used environmental controls for snake vivaria are rheostats and thermostats. Rheostats act as dimmers and need to be coordinated with thermometers to adjust light or heat output. They are commonly used with subtank heaters and ceramic infrared heating bulbs. Thermostats allow you to control basking site and substrate temperatures. Plug the heating units into the thermostat and set the desired temperature. Most thermostats have temperature probes, which should be positioned in the area where you want to achieve the set temperature (e.g., the basking site). The least expensive thermostats are on-off thermostats that turn on the heating unit when the temperature is below a set point and turn it off when the set-point is reached. More expensive, but also more precise, are pulse-proportional thermostats, which achieve the target temperature by effectively reducing or increasing the output of the heating device, rather than turning it on and off. Pulse-proportional thermostats are available through specialty reptile supply dealers and mail-order companies.

CHAPTER 12:

VIVARIA MAINTENANCE

Maintenance is the key to having an attractive display. Many factors will act against the order you had in mind, and only work will maintain or improve the envisioned design. In most cases, you need fifteen minutes a week to properly maintain a snake display. Plan for an additional half hour once a month for a major cleanup, including pruning or replacement of plants, rearrangement of landscape structures, and washing and disinfecting.

Fecal Matter

With the bioactive substrate system proposed, the standard procedure is to scoop out fecal masses using a cat litter scoop or strainer. Although in nature several processes and organisms break down fecal masses, this is not practical in small vivaria, in part because the arthropod species that break down fecal matter are not appealing to keepers. However, substrate bacteria will process whatever is not scooped. After removing fecal matter, stir the fouled area to mix it in with the deeper substrate layers. This exposes the waste matter to bacteria in the moist bacterial zone of the substrate.

For snakes from moist areas, mist daily or two to three times a week, depending on the species. With snakes from tropical forests, misting simulates natural processes, either rain or humidity fluctuations. Use purified water when misting your vivarium; it is mineral-free and will not stain glass. Misting will also drive water-soluble and water-carried substances below the surface of the substrate into the bioactive zone.

Once a week, be sure to do a general stirring of open substrate areas. This will help to prevent surface caking and to bury surface deposits.

Water Containers

Change water at least twice a week and whenever it is fouled. Wash the water container with a dish detergent solution and thoroughly rinse it before refilling. At least once a month, soak the container for a half hour in a 10-percent bleach solution to disinfect it, then thoroughly rinse before refilling. Always use high-quality drinking water, not purified water.

Tank Cleaning

The world tends toward entropy, so keeping order requires work either by physical and natural forces, biological organisms, or technology. Because the goal of keeping snakes is to have an aesthetic effect, you must work to maintain the desired order in the vivarium. Vivaria tend to get dirty; plants get damaged or become overgrown and snakes displace landscape structures. To keep a vivarium attractive, remove shed skin and rearrange and wash landscape structures when they become displaced or dirty. Prune and replace plants when necessary.

The top of the vivarium and light fixtures eventually get dusty and dirty. Regularly wipe the fixtures and top of the vivarium with a wet cloth or one sprayed with glass cleaner. Once a month, take the time to turn off the lights and inspect the undersides of fixtures and wipe them clean. Fluorescent tubes gather dust and benefit from regular wiping with a dust cloth.

Glass Cleaning

Keeping a tank attractive means once-a-week glass cleaning. Using a sprayer with purified water, spray the insides and use a small squeegee to clean the glass. If the water runs down into the substrate no harm will come of it, as long as you use only water. Use a single-edged razor to remove adhered dirt particles. If you use purified water to mist, there should be few, if any, mineral stains. Clean the outside glass with a commercial window cleaner, such as Windex.

Shedding

One snake-related phenomena that always attracts human attention is the process of skin shedding. All snakes shed their skins in one piece at intervals determined by a range of factors, including growth and sexual maturity, climatic and reproductive cycles, and state of health. For example, snakes with injured skin tend to shed more frequently. As a rule, fast-growing, young snakes shed more frequently than mature adults. Depending on the species, baby snakes raised in captivity can shed up to twelve times a year, sometimes more. Captive adult snakes shed less frequently, with many species shedding only six times a year and others as little as twice a year, after brumation/winter rest and, with females, right before laying eggs or giving birth.

The first sign that a snake is entering a shed cycle is a dulling of the skin and, soon after, an opaque white clouding of the eyes. This opaque stage is caused by the formation of a fluid between the live generating skin layer and the old, keratinized epidermal layer. The purpose of the fluid is to separate the two skin layers. When in the opaque stage of shedding, many snakes seek shelters or burrow in substrate. Some arboreal species may also come down to ground level. The purpose of this sheltering behavior is two-fold—to provide security during this vulnerable period when a snake's vision is impaired and to enter a more humid zone that will provide better conditions for extrusion of the old skin.

A snake usually does not feed during the shed cycle and should not be offered food. In addition, snakes in the shed cycle should not be handled because skin injuries may occur as the snake is generating a new epidermal layer. Snakes may also be more prone to striking during the opaque stage because of their impaired vision and a general sense of vulnerability.

The opaque stage is followed by a return to a clear-eyed stage and, after about a week, the snake will rub its snout against landscape structures. This detaches the old skin from the edges of the mouth and head. Finally, the snake slips out its old skin, which rolls off as the snake performs several activities that exert a pull on the loosened skin, helping to detach it. After shedding is completed, remove the dry shed skin from the enclosure.

Under certain conditions associated with low relative humidity, low substrate moisture, a desiccating substrate, or disease, snakes can have shedding difficulties. For more information on possible shedding disorders, see Diseases and Disorders.

CHAPTER 13:

SNAKE HANDLING

Most snake specialists are simply interested in observing snakes in an attractive enclosure and do not feel the need to handle their snakes. Still, many people want a snake that is both a display animal and a somewhat docile pet.

At the outset, if handling a snake is important to you, select species that are known to be docile and tolerant of handling, such as corn snakes, common kingsnakes, hognose snakes, rosy boas, ball pythons, and Colombian common boa constrictors. Many other snakes, even if initially prone to biting, usually grow out of it as they acclimate to the captive environment, as long as they are handled regularly. Remember, snakes have individual personalities, so they will vary in their aggressive tendencies and their propensity for fight-or-flight responses. Many rat snakes, water snakes, racers, carpet pythons, and green tree pythons are initially nippy but will settle down and tolerate some degree of handling. Some snake species are biters and even regular attempts at handling will not change their disposition. This is generally true of Amazon tree boas and can be true of some Texas rat snakes and jungle carpet pythons. These snakes stubbornly remain strikers and biters no matter how many bloodied attempts are made to handle them.

Picking Up Snakes

Before picking up a snake, assess its condition, attitude, and body posture. Snakes in shed, for example, have poor vision and are more likely to strike defensively. As a rule, do not handle snakes in shed. Hungry snakes are also prone to striking and should be first picked up with a snake hook under the front of the body to convey that the opening of their cage has nothing to do with feeding, even if that is what they are anticipating. A frightened, defensive snake will often adopt a characteristic prestrike posture and must be approached steadily or be encouraged to abandon a defensive posture by using a snake hook. Evaluate your snake before you reach for it or pick it up.

Snakes differ in their reaction to handling approaches. As a rule, steadily reaching for a snake is less likely to elicit a strike than hesitant jerky forward and backward motions. With regular handling, many snakes learn that the steady approach of a hand and arm is not threatening.

With larger snakes likely to cause some pain or injury with a bite, use a snake hook to gently lift the front of the body and elicit forward motion, guiding it into your hands. The use of a snake hook prior to handling creates a conditioning association with a harmless handling session.

If having a tame, easily handled snake is important to you, one or two brief weekly handling sessions—ten minutes or less—are beneficial to maintaining a positive, bite-free relationship with your snake.

Feeding-Response Conditioning

Snakebites often result from conditioning captive snakes to expect food whenever the owner opens the cage. This kind of conditioning occurs when owners get too busy to regularly handle their snakes or perform maintenance chores that require them to access the inside of an enclosure, so the vivarium is opened primarily to toss in food. Eventually, whenever the cage opens, the snake expects food and is ready to strike at any source of movement. To prevent this, maintain a regular handling or maintenance schedule to establish cage-access routines unassociated with feeding.

When handling or moving a snake, clearly define your intent by using a snake hook and lifting the front part of the body, encouraging the snake to move before handling or maintenance. Some keepers of large snakes always feed their snakes in separate containers to clearly differentiate feeding from activities performed in their display enclosure.

It is also worth noting that hungry snakes fed on an extended schedule are more apt to strike at moving objects. Well-fed snakes are not as likely to strike at any possible suggestion of food.

Hygiene

Snakes can harbor pathogens, such as parasites and salmonella strains, which can infect and cause illness in humans. Both LAM and bioactive substrates can harbor bacteria and parasites that will make you sick if ingested. For this reason, always practice common-sense hygiene when keeping snakes or any other reptile. Wash your hands after handling snakes and after performing maintenance chores. If you have many snakes and enclosures, wash and disinfect your hands between enclosures to prevent spreading disease. Good hygiene also means not allowing large snakes free run of a room, because they can smear fecal bacteria in parts of the home. Do not use household sinks and showers for snake maintenance or cleaning purposes; instead, designate a laundry or utility sink for your snakes. If you use a household sink, always clean and disinfect it after use.

Carefully supervise children when they handle your snakes to ensure they don't put their fingers in their mouths or kiss a snake in the course of handling. After handling, children must always wash their hands thoroughly with soap and water. Children are at special risk of contracting salmonellosis.

Tools

Several tools are useful for maintaining and handling different kinds of snakes. The following is an overview of the tools most commonly used by hobbyists.

Snake Hooks

The most useful tool for safely handling a snake is a snake hook. It allows you to pick up a snake, elevate part of its body, direct a snake, and, if necessary, pin down the head of an aggressive or dangerous snake. Commercially produced snake hooks come in a variety of sizes and are made of lightweight aluminum. They consist of a long rod and handle and a short 90-degree head, usually with a flattened tip. They come in various lengths to accommodate different size snakes.

Unless you keep only small and consistently docile species, a snake hook is a recommended tool for picking up possible biters, such as carpet pythons, tree boas, and some of the rat snakes. As a rule, do not use snake hooks to pin the heads of captive snakes, as this can be harmful if not done correctly.

Sexing Probes

With several species of snakes, accurate sexing is not readily possible without the use of sexing probes. These specially designed thin rods with rounded tips can be purchased from reptile supply dealers by mail order and at herpetological shows. All serious snake hobbyists own these tools to determine the sex of both adults and babies of a variety of species. Be sure to have their use demonstrated to you by a veterinarian or expert keeper to avoid causing injury.

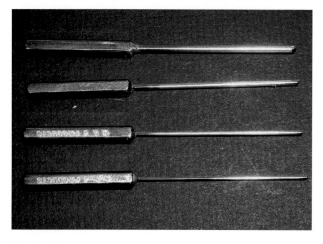

Shown is a set of sexing probes.

Feeding Forceps

These long tweezers allow you to offer prey items while keeping your hand outside of strike distance. They are recommended when offering food to most species. You can also use long forceps to remove shed skin from the cage.

A corn snake is sexed using a sexing probe.

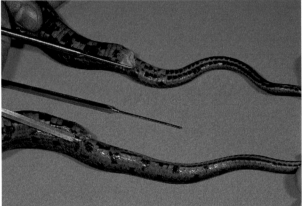

A sexing probe penetrates the caudal area to greater depth in males (bottom) than females (top).

Barbecue Tongs

An effective, easy-to-obtain, and sometimes-preferred alternative, tongs serve the same function as feeding forceps.

Pilstrom Tongs

Some snakes, such as tree boas and tree pythons, will not readily feed on dead prey unless it is moved or brought right up to their faces with forceps or tongs. With specimens that have a long strike range and can inflict a nasty bite, prekilled mice or rats can be offered at a safe distance using Pilstrom tongs. They can also be useful for removing uneaten prey without the risk of getting bitten.

With arboreal snakes that have a long strike range and long teeth, Pilstrom tongs work well for offering freshly killed prey.

Plastic Goggles

With arboreal or large, nasty snakes with a long strike range, wear clear plastic goggles or clear glasses so you are not accidentally bitten in the eye. A bite to the eye can be serious, resulting in a torn eyelid or worse. Although bites to the eye are very rare, there is one case on record of an individual whose frightened pet boa struck and embedded its teeth through his eyelid and into the eyeball. Emergency medical technicians were called. The snake was decapitated and surgery was required to remove the embedded head. The individual had impaired vision and could have lost sight in one eye. Simply wearing some type of glasses can help prevent this kind of accident.

Plastic Shields

To avoid being bitten by strike-prone snakes, a clear plastic shield, assembled by attaching a handle to a pane of Plexiglas, allows you to block a nasty snake while doing maintenance. You can also place a freestanding, clear, plastic barrier in front of the snake while working in the enclosure.

Leather Gloves

Wear leather work gloves when handling medium-sized species that tend to writhe, release musk, bite, or fail to remain on a snake hook. With gloved hands, smaller snakes can be grabbed around the midbody and held during transfer from one container to another. I have found leather work gloves useful with some of the water snakes, including rear-fanged species, as well as young Cook's tree boas and nippy carpet pythons. Wear a long sleeve shirt and keep the snakes away from your face.

CHAPTER 14:

DIET

One of the great advantages of snakes as pets and display animals is that they are low-maintenance captives compared to most vertebrate animals. This is due primarily to their feeding habits and their particular patterns of activity and metabolism. Indeed, many of the snakes commonly kept in captivity will live long and healthy lives when offered only one or two prey items every one to three weeks.

Snakes are carnivores that consume whole prey. The species most commonly kept in captivity feed on vertebrates, primarily commercially raised mice and rats, or fish in the case of garter snakes and water snakes. Most of the snakes covered in this book feed readily in captivity and present few problems.

Rodent-Eating Snakes

In captivity, rodent-eating snakes are usually offered commercially bred mice and rats. These are available either live or prekilled and frozen through many pet stores and specialized reptile stores. You can order frozen mice and rats in quantity (clear out a section of your freezer) from mail-order companies. Because snakes eat whole prey, feeding is simple. There are no recipes, no food preparation, and, in most cases, no supplementation required. A whole prey item fills all of a snake's dietary needs.

Try to find suppliers that offer mice and rats fed on laboratory rodent blocks or chow. These are more likely to contain sufficient levels of essential or beneficial nutrients, such as vitamin C. Avoid buying obese, retired adult mice and rats and focus on obtaining leaner prey items. Feeding obese prey can cause steatitis (inflamed fat deposits under the skin), obesity, and other health problems in snakes.

Feeding Live or Dead Prey

The great majority of rodent-eating snakes will feed on, or can be trained to feed on, dead prey, either freshly killed or previously frozen. This is an option increasingly preferred by snake keepers for a variety of reasons. First, it's more humane for the prey. Commercial rodent suppliers utilize humane techniques, such as carbon dioxide gas or spinal dislocation. This spares snake owners from having to kill prey or watch prey be killed by their snake. It also prevents the risk of a live rat or mouse gnawing on a snake.

Frozen prekilled mice or rats can be conveniently stored in large numbers in the freezer, avoiding frequent trips to a store. Moreover, you avoid the expense and effort of keeping and feeding rodents, and enduring rodent smells. All you need to do is remove the frozen prey item from its plastic baggie, allow it to thaw thoroughly and warm to room temperature, then offer it to your snake.

Some snakes, however, are reluctant to feed on thawed, dead rodents. The prey needs to be warm or moving for them to be interested. Some tricks can convince these picky feeders include: 1) warm previously frozen prey under an incandescent bulb; 2) offer a freshly killed prey item that is still warm; and 3) offer the prey off forceps with an occasional jiggle. Still, depending on the species, there are some snakes that will only accept live prey of the right type. I have found this to be the case with babies of a variety of species, including some rat snakes and kingsnakes, diadem snakes, racers, Pacific boas, and green tree pythons. In addition, many imported adult tree boas and pythons, diadem snakes, vine snakes, and a variety of lizard-eating species initially only show interest in live prey. If a snake consistently refuses to feed on dead prey, the only resort is to offer it live food.

Size of Prey

The key limiting factor, in terms of prey size, is girth. If the prey is too large, a snake will not be able to swallow it; if it is ingested, the meal may be regurgitated. The prey item should have a body width one to one and a half times the width of a snake at mid-body. Using this gauge, one to two prey items can be offered per feeding. Some baby snakes (such as carpet pythons and green tree pythons) are more likely to start feeding on prey that is relatively large, with a girth two to three times the snake's mid-body girth.

How to Feed

Offer small terrestrial and semiarboreal snakes prekilled prey on a bare area of substrate or on a solid surface, such as a flat rock. You can also offer the prey item using forceps or tongs. Forceps are recommended with all arboreal species because many are reluctant to feed on dead prey placed on the ground. Instead, the prey may need to be jiggled to simulate movement and draw attention. For your safety, use long tongs such as the Pilstrom tongs or trash-grabbing tongs sold in hardware stores with large snakes that have a long strike range, such as adult carpet pythons, boa constrictors, emerald tree boas, and Amazonian tree boas. This will prevent the risk of being bitten while offering food.

Depending on the species, multiple snakes kept in the same enclosure may need to be removed and fed individually in plastic storage containers or trashcans with secure lids. If the mice are placed at the opposite ends of the snakes' enclosure, some rodent-eating species can be fed in the same vivaria without fights occurring.

Most snakes will accept prekilled prey.

Feeding Schedules and Growth

The standard feeding schedule in the snake-keeping hobby is once a week. If a snake hibernates for three to four months out of a year, this means that a snake requires thirty to forty-six meals a year. However, many vertebrate-eating snakes in the wild survive on a fraction of this amount; with most species it is possible to keep them in good condition with meals every ten to fourteen days, or twenty-two to thirty times a year. Some snakes, such as diamond pythons, fare best on a lower feeding regimen, as few as ten meals a year. One effect of a reduced feeding regime is that snakes take longer to grow and mature and tend to produce fewer eggs (or neonates) per clutch. If your primary interest is to breed large numbers of snakes then definitely stay on a once-a-week feeding schedule with females of most snakes. Studies have shown that the breeding potential of female snakes is directly related to their relative weight/energy reserves. On the other hand, leaner, more slowly grown snakes are more active and do not suffer from obesity or breeding problems such as egg-binding. They may also end up living longer than the stuffed sausages that are now increasingly common in our hobby.

I find that the captive-raised snakes I purchase appear fat, almost bloated, so I maintain them on a reduced feeding regimen to allow them to gradually lose weight and achieve optimal condition. To determine when to feed your snake, try waiting until it shows the high activity level associated with hunting for at least one day. Remember, however, most snakes are crepuscular and nocturnal, so this high activity level is often observable only at night. After they have captured food and are satiated, snakes usually enter a period of energy-conserving, reduced activity that may include basking to hasten digestion.

Under my lean feeding regimen, snakes grow at a rate that corresponds closely (given improved feeding efficiency at lower rates) to the difference in feeding schedule, because less calories in a given period of time means less growth and less weight gained. Because my regime is one-third to one-half the standard weekly regime, snakes raised under this schedule take almost twice as long to reach sexual maturity as "power-fed" specimens. With some species, we have conducted experiments where snakes were fed every two to three weeks. They required up to three times longer to mature than snakes kept under an intensive weekly feeding regimen. These slow-grown snakes tend to more closely match the maturity time and growth rates of snakes in the wild.

Adjust the meal size or frequency to achieve the desired appearance. If a snake appears unusually thin, then increase the feeding schedule or the size or amount of prey items per feeding. One of the negative consequences of an extended feeding regime is that hungry snakes tend to be more active and more prone to striking and biting.

A small kingsnake constricts a mouse prior to feeding.

Pampering and Good Displays

If you provide a snake with everything it needs all the time—including food—the results will be inactivity and obesity. Snakes that feel cool emerge and spend time basking and snakes that are hungry often start to hunt. A snake provided the perfect temperature, comfort of a shelter, and frequent regular feeding will spend most of its time concealed and inactive. As we know, the easy way is not always the best way. Overcoming hardships can make one stronger and more interesting—this goes for snakes, too.

Water Snakes and Garter Snakes

Feed water snakes and garter snakes once a week or they will lose weight. Offer goldfish or other live foods in a feeding container with a low level of water or in the water section of an aqua-terrarium. Although some claim that goldfish can carry parasites that harm water snakes and garter snakes, I have individuals that have been raised on goldfish for more than seven years and they are healthy and breed annually.

An alternative is to feed fresh fish fillets of low-fat fish species and coat them with a calcium/vitamin mineral supplement (two parts calcium to one part reptile multi-vitamin/mineral powder (2:1). Some additional food preparation is also recommended when feeding fish. Both marine and freshwater fish can contain significant amounts of the enzyme thiaminase, which is an enzyme that destroys vitamin B_1. Snakes with vitamin B_1 deficiencies demonstrate neurological signs, including convulsions and seizures, and will die if not treated promptly (consult a qualified veterinarian for a vitamin B_1 injection). John Rossi, D.V.M., author of *What's Wrong with My Snake?* (1996), recommends freezing fish to help kill parasites then warming them up (176° F for five minutes) to destroy the enzyme thiaminase. Finally, supplement with a vitamin B_1 source.

In vivaria with particulate substrates (sand and soil rather than newspaper), it is best to remove fish-eating snakes from the enclosure and feed them individually in separate plastic terrariums. If fed in the vivarium, cover the open substrate area with newspaper and place the food on top. Water snakes, even if fish are placed in the water container, will pull their prey out of the water and swallow the fish on land. This will cause substrate to adhere to the wet fish, resulting in the snake swallowing substrate or releasing the soil-covered fish.

Garter snakes and water snakes, which typically feed on fish and amphibians, can also be tricked into taking prekilled mice by rubbing the backs of mice with a piece of cut fish.

Rough Green Snakes
Insect-eating snakes, such as rough green snakes, should be fed crickets of the appropriate size (length of cricket body equal to length of the head of the snake) at least twice a

Water snakes and garter snakes readily feed on live feeder fish.

week. As with insectivorous lizards, the crickets should be lightly coated (just a light dusted appearance not a powder-coated look) with a reptile vitamin/mineral powder. Most hobbyists use a two-to-one (2:1) or three-to-one (3:1) ratio of calcium carbonate to reptile multivitamin/mineral powder mix. A pinch of the mix is added in a jar containing crickets of the appropriate size. After a few gentle swirls to lightly coat the crickets, drop them into the vivarium.

Lizard Feeders

Several species of snakes feed primarily on lizards when young and into adulthood. Many baby colubrids and boids start as lizard or frog feeders, but graduate to warm-blooded prey as adults. Vine snakes are almost exclusively lizard eaters at all sizes. Snakes that eat lizards tend to be attracted to both smell and motion, so it is best to offer them live lizards.

Green anoles, because they are so readily available, continue to be the lizard of choice for lizard eaters. This poses no problem as long as anoles are regularly available. The main problem with anoles is that they are often parasitized, so ideally they should be deparasitized prior to feeding. When possible, switch snakes to a rodent diet by scenting pink (newborn mice) or fuzzy (older mice that have grown fur) mice with the skin of a lizard (a dead lizard can be frozen for this purpose). Alternatively, breed one or more prolific lizard species to maintain a consistent

121

supply of healthy lizards as food. Geckos, such as Turkish geckos and leopard geckos, are possible candidates, as are bearded dragons (although the idea of feeding captive-bred lizards to snakes is often more disturbing to reptile owners than offering mice and rats).

Problem Feeders

Snakes that refuse to feed do so for a number of reasons. The environmental conditions may be inadequate (too low temperature or lack of shelter), they may be sick or brumating (a fasting period during the winter or in rare cases during warm summer temperatures), or the wrong type of food may be offered. Each of these possibilities needs to be addressed. If a snake that is healthy and kept under the right conditions does not feed during the warm seasons of the year (spring and summer), then prey selection might be the cause of food refusal.

The great majority of snakes presented in this book readily feed on mice or rats of the appropriate size. With some species, such as gray-banded kingsnakes or Pacific ground boas, it is difficult to start juveniles on mice. In some cases, you may need to make several weekly attempts offering live baby mice in a small container before a baby snake decides to feed. In other cases, a prekilled baby mouse with its skull crushed and brain matter smeared on the head can elicit feeding. Some baby snakes of species that eat rodents as adults stubbornly refuse to feed on mice when young. An effective method to get them started is a process called scenting, during which a prekilled baby mouse is washed in water, dried, and rubbed with a dead lizard or with the shed-skin of a lizard. There will be some species or individuals where only offering a live lizard will initiate feeding.

Some species of snakes specialize in eating frogs or toads. A prekilled mouse or young rat may have to be scented by rubbing the skin of a live or dead toad or frog on its back. This method works well for initiating feeding on mice in eastern hognose snakes (specialized toad eaters).

See particular species sections for additional feeding information.

Drinking Water

The availability of clean water is essential for the welfare of most snakes. There are currently a variety of water containers for reptiles available in the pet trade. Most are made of molded plastic and many simulate rock. Alternatives include shallow, plastic food-storage containers or small dog bowls. For larger snakes, provide larger bowls or plastic storage containers. Some snakes, such as water snakes and garter snakes, should have water containers large enough for them to immerse their entire bodies. As a guideline, the height of a water container should be two to three times the thickness of a snake's body.

The water provided to snakes should be of a drinking quality suitable for humans. Low chlorine levels, as found in the tap water of many areas, are considered safe for most snakes. Replace water at least twice a week and whenever it is fouled. Most snakes will not drink from a fouled water container, so they risk dehydration if clean water is unavailable. Even water that appears clear may have high bacterial or algae levels if it is not replaced regularly and the container is not cleaned.

Misting

Various tropical forest species benefit from a light daily misting to raise relative humidity. Misting can also stimulate activity in several species, including tropical, arboreal snakes such as emerald tree pythons and green tree pythons. In some species, such as Asian vine snakes (*Ahaetulla* sp.),

A variety of plastic water containers that simulate rock are offered in the pet trade.

misting generates water droplets that allow the snakes to recognize water and drink. There are currently a number of misting systems available to hobbyists. The least expensive and most widely used misters are hand sprayers and manual pump sprayers available through hardware stores, nurseries, and department stores. You can also purchase more expensive automatic misting systems regulated by timers. No matter what system is used, the duration of misting should be limited and adjusted to prevent the substrate from becoming soggy or waterlogged; otherwise you will have to devise a drainage system with a subtank sump pump. With the BSS system, waterlogging kills aerobic bacteria and causes a rise in anaerobic species, along with a foul stench.

For species that drink from water droplets, hand mist directly around the area of the mouth while the snake is performing drinking motions to assure it gets enough water while minimizing soaking of the display. Also, place a water-collecting container below the area being sprayed to prevent water-logging the substrate. Use purified water when misting to prevent the accumulation of mineral stains on the sides of your enclosures and plants. All misting equipment should be washed and disinfected on a regular, monthly basis. Over time, the insides of misters develop an algal and bacterial coat. With automatic systems, flush and disinfect lines regularly; bacteria, possibly pathogenic, can grow on the inside lining of hoses and pipes.

Hand sprayers are useful for misting small numbers of cages. For a large number of enclosures, or room-sized enclosures, manual pump-type sprayers are more effective and less tedious to use.

CHAPTER 15:

BREEDING

Anyone involved in keeping animals will have questions about whether they should be kept in pairs or groups and whether they should be given the opportunity to reproduce. Many hobbyists also wonder about their responsibility to propagate rare species or unusually attractive forms and the potential financial rewards such endeavors may bring.

At the outset, let me say that it is perfectly fine to keep only a single snake or a pair of snakes for display. Many snakes sold in the pet trade are now captive-bred by the hundreds or thousands, depending on the species, so they are not rare in captivity. Nonetheless, snake hobbyists often develop an interest in breeding the species they maintain. After all, keeping a pair of snakes is not much more trouble than keeping one. Breeding your snakes also gives you the pleasure of seeing babies born and, in some cases, the surprise birth of unusually attractive individuals. It allows

A gray-banded kingsnake *(Lampropeltis alterna)* hatches. Snakes usually do not emerge until several hours after slitting an egg. Allow them to come out on their own.

you to acquire new animals and sometimes sell the excess offspring to offset the expenses of your hobby. This is fine as long as you limit the number of animals you keep and resist the temptation to go into large-scale production.

Commercially breeding snakes on a large scale will set you on a path incongruous with the art of keeping snakes because it requires that you adopt the LAM space- and labor-saving methods. Before long, like most large-scale breeders, you will spend all of your free time cleaning and feeding and will not have the time to enjoy your snakes. The snakes that once fascinated you become products.

Think carefully before you decide on the course of commercial snake breeding. Making an income from breeding snakes is increasingly difficult and competitive. It requires business and management skills as well as long-term planning. Every year there are hundreds of snake hobbyists and breeders, who, disillusioned, decide that breeding snakes is not worth the time and hassle and end

A baby rat snake's hemipenes are manually eversed. Experience is required to do this without harming the snake.

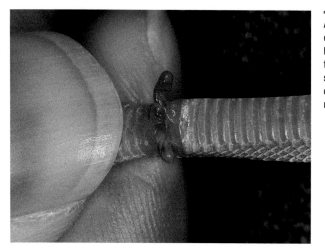

After manual eversion of the hemipenes, this baby rat snake turned out to be a male.

up selling their entire collections. What started off as something enjoyable ended up a burden.

If you love snakes and want to breed them, limit the numbers to what can be maintained in four hours a week or less. Beyond that, you will no longer be able to appreciate your individual animals. Business, rather than art, will become the focus of your hobby.

The focus of this book is display and not production, so I have included only a brief outline of the snake breeding process. If interested in breeding snakes, consult one of the many books on the keeping and breeding of specific snakes.

You must have at least one sexually mature, healthy pair of snakes. Some species, such as several of the boas and ball pythons, are more likely to breed successfully if multiple males are available or if they are kept in groups. Consider this when assembling your breeding stock. With most species, males and females are kept separately most of the year except for breeding introductions.

Prebreeding Conditioning: Brumation

Most temperate and subtropical species should have a winter rest/brumation period lasting two to four months, during which time they are kept cooler and drier and are not fed. In the wild, seasonal changes reduce temperatures in the winter, when snakes often remain inactive and with-

Most snakes will breed in late winter or early spring, at the end of a period of brumation/hibernation that combines both cooling and fasting. This pair of corn snakes is copulating.

out appetite for extended periods. With snakes from temperate or subtropical areas, winter-related reductions in temperature and photoperiod contribute to what snake keepers call winter shutdown, in which a snake enters a period of inactivity and fasting. This rest period at cooler temperatures is essential for health, longevity, and inducing the breeding cycle in snake species.

Before Cooling

Prior to winter cool down, examine your snakes to make sure they are healthy and in optimal condition. Do not cool down sick or very thin snakes. About two weeks prior to the cool down period, stop feeding snakes to ensure their intestines are cleared of digested food. With cool temperatures, undigested food in the gut risks decomposition (bacterial, rather than digestive). The speed of movement through the gut will be reduced at cool temperatures and there can be an increased risk of disease because of microbial imbalances and a depressed immune system.

Snake species have varying requirements for winter cool down; hobbyists should consult books that refer to the species they maintain. In captivity, the general procedure for cooling down temperate snakes is to turn off heating devices and reduce the photoperiod to ten hours a day, starting sometime after October 15. Place the setups or hibernation containers in an area where the temperature drops below 65° F during the day and into the 50s at night. Because it is inconvenient to move an entire setup, many keepers remove snakes from their display enclosures and transfer them to large, plastic storage boxes with holes drilled in the side to provide airflow. Place newspaper or aspen shaving substrate on the bottom of the box, along with a container of water. Secure the lid on the box with large rubber bands, Velcro straps, or tape. Place the box on a shelf in a room that reaches the desired temperature range.

Some montane or more northern species of snakes require more drastic cooling into the low 50s to breed successfully. A few snakes, such as indigo snakes, actually breed during the cool period rather than after warm-up, and should be hibernated in pairs in large enclosures. Depending on the species, winter cool down should last from three to four months. Do not feed your animals during the entire cool down period, but always provide clean water. Check the animals at least every other week to make sure the conditions in the hibernation containers are adequate and that the snakes do not show signs of disease, such as severe weight loss, gaping, bubbly mucus emerging from the sides of the mouth, or weakness and limpness. Any snake showing signs of disease should be immediately removed from the cool area, returned to normal conditions with a basking spot, and treated as needed.

Many tropical species only require small winter drops in temperature, between 5° F and 10° F. These conditions are easily achieved in most households during the winter. Subtank heaters can be rheostatically or thermostatically adjusted to provide the lower temperatures. Reduce the wattage of spotlight bulbs so that basking site temperatures are 77-80° F. The typical procedure for tropical snakes, such as many of the boas and pythons, is to subject them to 10° F night drops and 5° F daytime drops.

With most snakes, you can return vivarium conditions to normal beginning sometime between March 1 and April 1. Offer snakes food about a week after resuming warmer conditions.

Breeding

One to two weeks after returning to the normal maintenance schedule, introduce the female to the male. Some breeders alternate introducing and removing females for a week at a time.

The female's first spring shed following return to normal conditions is usually the optimal breeding period. During that time, the skin of a freshly shed female may contain pheromones that can elicit courtship and breeding by males. Introduce the female and her shed skin into the male's cage as soon as shedding is completed. After copulation has been observed and the female no longer appears receptive, return her to her regular enclosure. Once gravid, the female will gradually appear more swollen and will eventually stop feeding. The female will usually shed again as she nears egg-laying. Once the eggs are shelled and ready to be laid, they often become individually defined and their outlines visible against the body wall of the snake.

A close-up of copulating Honduran milk snakes shows the insertion of the hemipenis into the female cloaca.

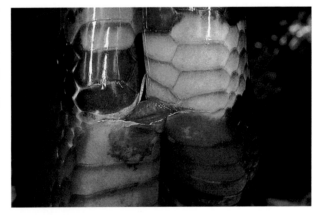

Egg-Laying

With egg-laying species, use a laying box made from a bucket or a plastic storage box that is large enough for the female to coil in, with an access hole in the side. Fill the container half-full with moist (not wet) peat moss and place it in the enclosure. In most cases, females will decide to nest in the box. In other cases, the female may lay inside another shelter or under landscape structures in the vivarium.

Snake eggs can be successfully incubated in a variety of moist media, including sphagnum moss (left) and vermiculite (right).

Incubation

After the clutch is laid, remove the eggs from the vivarium. If adhered together, remove the egg mass in the position it was laid; do not separate the eggs. Then, transfer the eggs to plastic storage containers that have aeration holes on the sides and are partially filled (usually a layer about twice the width of an egg) with a layer of moistened vermiculite or perlite (four parts medium to three parts water by weight, not volume (4:3)). Bury the eggs in the moist medium, leaving one-half to one-third of the upper portion exposed. Then, place the egg containers inside thermostat-controlled incubators. Most colubrid eggs are incubated between 76° and 86° F, and python eggs are incubated between 88° F

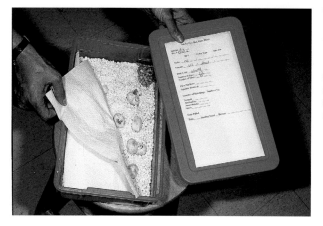

Reptile eggs are often incubated in perlite, a porous substrate that allows good airflow and moisture.

A stinking goddess rat snake *(Elaphe carinata)* is wrapped around a just-laid clutch of eight eggs.

and 90° F. With both groups, maintain the eggs at 80 to 90 percent humidity. Most snake eggs hatch after sixty to seventy days of incubation, but this can vary quite a bit depending on species and incubation conditions.

With live-bearing snakes, particularly boas, provide a basking site with the surface temperature reaching 88-92° F. Gestation, depending on environmental conditions and species, can range from as little as seven weeks for some Floridian forms of garter snakes and water snakes, up to ten months for some of the boas.

Tropical Species

Tropical species require only slight cooling during the winter, a 5–10° F drop in temperature for two to three months.

A corn snake is coiled around its eggs in a nest box lined with moist vermiculite.

Some breeders allow daytime temperatures to climb up to around 80° F but lower the nighttime temperature to 70-72° F. Exceptionally cool winter temperatures can cause tropical species to become sick, usually with respiratory infections. Research the techniques used by tropical species specialists to cool and precondition their snakes. For tropical snakes, the photoperiod is reduced to ten hours; food is withheld for most species. Several tropical snakes are kept in breeding groups during the winter cooling period because breeding may occur during this time.

Record Keeping

Keeping records of your snakes' behaviors can be a source of valuable information. Serious snake hobbyists record the air temperature of the setup, the birthdates of individual snakes, when a snake feeds, when it defecates, and when it sheds. If you are interested specifically in growth, record the weight of the prey items, and, on a monthly basis, the length and weight of the snake. If interested in breeding behaviors, then note feeding, copulation times, period between noted copulation and egg laying, and shedding patterns. For example, most snake species shed their skin a certain number of days or weeks prior to egg-laying or giving birth.

With the art of keeping snakes, additional information can be noted, including behaviors in relation to basking sites, cooler temperatures, shelters, substrate, and the changes in barometric pressure associated with rainstorms. For example, hungry snakes tend to be active but after they have eaten spend extended periods of time in a shelter or coiled over or near a hot spot or basking site. Snakes in shed usually stay at ground level and hide in shelters or partially burrow in substrate. A sign that snakes are adapting to captivity is that they start forming behavioral patterns.

CHAPTER 16:

DISEASES AND DISORDERS

O nce established and maintained within the proper husbandry parameters, many captive snakes are remarkably problem free. Diseases are most likely to occur with newly purchased nonestablished animals, or as a result of changes in environmental conditions. Imported wild-collected snakes are often parasite infected, and in some cases may harbor more serious diseases that will require quarantine and urgent veterinary treatment.

As a snake keeper, you should always be on the lookout for possible signs of disease. Regularly check on your animals and, when possible, keep records of their activity, feeding, and weight. Many of the snake diseases detected in established animals are precipitated by improper husbandry. Thus, when you first notice signs of illness,

The banded wart snake is a brackish water species and requires about a tablespoon of salt per gallon of water. High ammonia and nitrite levels will result in a potentially fatal skin blister disease.

immediately evaluate the husbandry conditions. Keeping snakes too cool, too hot, too dry, or too wet are the most common husbandry related causes of disease. During the winter, respiratory infections are the most frequently seen disease in tropical snakes kept too cool.

Remember that with ectotherms the efficiency of the immune system is linked to metabolic rate, which is affected by temperature. A snake kept in the wrong temperature range is more prone to infection. With some snakes, the wrong kind of landscaping, such as a lack of shelter or shaded perches, can cause stress that will result in a disinterest in food, weight loss, and gradual decline. With others, stress from overcrowding can be a contributing factor to the onset of disease.

Prevention

Nothing is more valuable for maintaining a healthy collection than following procedures to prevent the onset and spread of disease. If you have more than one snake, quarantine is the first preventative measure. Even if you keep only one snake in a naturalistic vivarium, you may want to first quarantine the snake in a simple LAM-type setup to prevent the spread of possible parasites or pathogens in the vivarium and to reduce the risks of reinfection. With some diseases, such as mite infestations or coccidiosis, you must dismantle and disinfect the entire setup. It is best to recognize and treat disease before introduction to a naturalistic vivarium rather than after.

The next most important preventative measure is good husbandry, meaning providing the right enclosure, temperature range, relative humidity, and landscape structures, as well as regular water availability and feeding.

Veterinarians

Although I commonly recommend that reptile hobbyists use the services of veterinarians, you must make the effort to find a qualified and competent reptile veterinarian. Veterinarians inexperienced with reptiles can misdiagnose signs of illness, provide improper treatment and husbandry recommendations, and cause more harm than good—in addition to wasting your money.

To find a qualified reptile veterinarian, talk to other hobbyists, members of herpetological societies, or personnel of reptile stores. Ask them to help you identify veterinarians in your area with a good reputation for treating reptiles. The Association of Reptile and Amphibian Veterinarians (ARAV) maintains a list of members and can also provide you with the names of specialized reptile veterinarians in your state.

After a consultation with a veterinarian, evaluate the costs of treatment and limit the amount to what you can reasonably afford. In my opinion, very sick snakes—unless rare or valuable—are generally best euthanized, particularly if you own a large collection. The time and costs involved in certain treatments and the potential risks to a collection should always be considered. Nature tends to eliminate the weak and very sick early in the game; hobbyists should follow this model to prevent the increase and spread of virulent diseases.

That said, I recommend an initial veterinary exam and treatment for parasites with all wild-collected snakes. With captive-bred snakes that appear healthy, a quarantine period allows you to notice signs of obvious problems or illness, such as weight loss or runny stools, which require veterinary treatment.

Common Diseases and Disorders

Rostral Abrasion

Rostral abrasion is the term used to describe injury to the end of the snout due to rubbing or pressing it against a screen top or abrasive areas of a cage. It is usually associated with some form of stress. A snake wants out of the conditions it's kept in or is lacking conditions that make it feel comfortable. Causes include too warm or too small an enclosure, and failure to provide shelters or other landscape structures. Excessive vibrations and noise generated by loud music can also be stressful for captive snakes and overcrowding can trigger restlessness. In any case, rostral abrasion is a sign that a change in environmental conditions is necessary. It must be addressed as quickly as possible to prevent further injury. With minor abrasions, apply antibiotic ointment to the exposed area. In severe cases where the tissues of the snout are swollen, raw, or infected, consult a veterinarian for treatment with antibiotics.

Mites

Mites, tiny blood sucking acarids, are the most common external parasites encountered in captive snakes. Because of their life cycle and habits, they can be difficult to eradicate in collections and their numbers can quickly increase to life-threatening levels. For this reason, snake owners should be methodical in implementing prevention practices, including quarantining all new snakes, preventative treatment with a miticide, and careful hygiene procedures. Always wash hands and change clothes after touching any objects in a room with mite-infested snakes. As a rule, carefully examine new snakes for the presence of mites and keep them in a room separate from your collection during quarantine.

Mites, if they are present in large numbers, are easily noticed on snakes. The mites themselves appear as tiny, beadlike, dark red bugs crawling on the skin of the snake or in some cases on the sides of the tank or landscape structures. They can also be seen lodged in the corners of snake eyes, causing a slight lifting of the eye rim. Because mite-infested snakes often spend large amounts of time soaking coiled in a water container, you may notice drowned mites at the bottom of the container, looking like tiny black specks. Another sign of mites is the presence of bright white fine speckling on the snake's skin, actually mite feces.

To treat for mites, place the snake in a separate enclosure, either a bare glass tank with screen top or a large plastic storage container with multiple ventilation holes. Spray the snake with an ivermectin solution, (5 to 10 mg of ivermectin (Ivomec) per quart) and keep it in isolation in a LAM setup. Treat it again every five days, for a total of four treatments, to make sure all mites are dead. Other methods for treating mites include the application of a pyrethrin-based flea powder after placing the snake in a well-ventilated container, or overnight exposure to a section of insecticidal strip. A 1- by 2-inch section of an insecticidal strip will effectively treat snakes in a 20-gallon vivarium, with the screen top partially covered. After twenty-four hours remove the strip and store it in plastic wrap, then repeat the treatment in seven to ten days.

A big problem with mites is reinfestation. Mites may lay their eggs away from the host and can wander out of a cage, basically putting themselves out of range of most treatments. Preventing reinfestation means first killing any mites in the cage, which, if it is a naturalistic setup, means removing the snake and placing a sizeable piece of insecticide strip in the enclosure then sealing the top by taping plastic sheeting over it. This kills mites and many of the other arthropods in the setup and can harm some plants. At least three days of treatment are required for the vaporized miticide to reach all the nooks and crannies where mites may be hiding. Repeat the treatment twice at ten-day intervals. In addition, spray the outside of the cage with an ivermectin solution and wipe all surrounding furniture with a cloth moistened with a cleaning solution like Windex. Keep the snake in a separate enclosure and treat it for mites during this period.

If it sounds like a big pain to effectively treat mites, then you will appreciate the importance of quarantine in a LAM setup and preventative treatment with a miticide before introducing a snake into a vivarium.

Ticks

Ticks are external parasitic acarids that are almost exclusively seen on wild-collected snakes. Some species, such as ball pythons, commonly harbor ticks while others are usually tick free. Ticks appear as flat, scalelike creatures embedded in the skin between scales. Because ticks may serve as vectors for spreading certain diseases, they should always be removed when noticed. To do this, simply grab the tick body firmly with tweezers and yank it out. Drop the tick in a container with rubbing alcohol to kill it. To prevent the risk of infection at the removal site, apply a disinfectant or antibiotic ointment.

Shedding Problems

Healthy snakes kept under the proper conditions will shed their skin in one piece without any problems. The failure to shed properly, characterized by varying amounts of retained adhering skin, is usually due to dry conditions (low relative humidity or a desiccated substrate) or illness. Sick snakes, because they are weak, have difficulty performing the activity required to remove shed skin. Dehydrated snakes, whether from illness or lack of water, may also have problems shedding. In some cases snakes will successfully shed their skin but their eyecaps, the portion of epithelial skin that covers the surface of the eye, remain adhered.

To remove dried, adhering shed skin, soak the snake in a ventilated (with holes) plastic storage container with a small amount of water, a depth equal to half the diameter of the snake's body. After four to six hours, remove the snake. The skin should be soft and easily slide off. Keepers also suggest putting the snake in a ventilated plastic storage box with wet newspaper or wet sponges for it to crawl through.

During the shedding cycle the skin turns a milky white, then clears up a few days prior to the actual shedding of the old skin. During this period, mist emerald trees boas and other tropical arboreal snakes with lukewarm water daily.

Eyecaps that fail to shed will give the eyes a slightly opaque, raised, and dried look. Gently grasp the snake and examine its eyes; you will see the thickening that indicates a retained eyecap. Pushing down gently with a fingernail at the edge of the eye rim should allow you to see the edge of the retained eye cap, looking like dried skin. The first step is to soften it using the soak method mentioned above. Then, find the edge of the skin. First, try gently lifting the edge with a fingernail. Once a section of eyecap is lifted, it can be grabbed between fingernails or round-nosed tweezers and gently peeled off. This should only be done after a snake has attempted to shed and only if you are certain there is an adhering eye cap. If you do this while a snake is shedding or attempt to remove a non-existent eye cap, you risk damaging the eye(s) of your snake and possibly cause blindness. If you are unsure, visit your veterinarian.

Skin Blister Disease

Raised, whitish, pimplelike areas on the dorsal skin or brownish or reddish discolored scales on the belly characterize this disease. It is caused by conditions that allow skin infection by pathogenic bacteria. The usual causes are an environment that is too cool and moist or a foul, wet substrate. Both provide ideal conditions for the growth of pathogenic bacteria, but poor conditions for the beneficial

A carpet python exhibits incomplete shedding due to too low humidity.

substrate bacteria that normally act probiotically. Skin blister disease occurs on soggy, cool substrates but seldom, if ever, in snakes kept on an airy, moist, warm bioactive substrate. The best way to avoid the disease is to prevent the soggy, cool conditions conducive to it. If noticed early, skin blister disease can be treated by topical application of a dilute antiseptic solution (Betadine) solution or an antibiotic ointment. Keep the affected snake in a LAM setup on dry newspaper at optimal warm temperatures, depending on the species, until cured. In cases with signs of extensive infection or when no improvement is noted, bring the affected snake to a qualified veterinarian for administration of antibiotics. Untreated, this disease can become systemic and be fatal.

Mouth Problems

The most common mouth problem of snakes is stomatitis, popularly known as "mouth rot." This is a bacterial infection that results in swelling and reddening of the gums and the accumulation of white caseous material (solidified pus). In time, teeth may fall out and the jawbone may be affected. The first signs are usually slightly protruding labials (scales forming the edge of the mouth), which when pulled back reveal an area of reddening or cheesy white matter.

To treat, apply diluted hydrogen peroxide, antiseptic solution, or antiseptic mouthwash (Listerine) topically to affected areas twice a day, using a cotton swab. Remove loose teeth. Keep the snake in a LAM-type setup, with a hot spot between 85° F and 90° F, until well. Stomatitis can be infectious, so isolate the snake during treatment. Too low temperatures, stress, overcrowding, and an unsuitable environment are probably contributing factors. If the infection is extensive, teeth are falling out, and the jawbone seems infected, consult a veterinarian immediately for treatment with antibiotics.

Failure to Feed and Weight Loss

Because snakes may refuse food at different times for

different reasons, a failure to feed must be interpreted in the context of environmental conditions and other signs related to health. For example, it is normal for a snake to fast when it is in shed, during winter cool down, during breeding, and in the latter stages of the gestation period. During normal fasting, which occurs during winter cool down or breeding, weight loss is minimal and easily regained once feeding is resumed. On the other hand, many diseases eventually lead to a failure to feed and significant weight loss.

Internal Parasites

Weight loss, inability to gain weight, failure to feed, soft or runny feces, blood in the feces, and worms in the feces are all signs of possible infection by internal parasites. The only solution is to have a fecal exam performed by a qualified veterinarian and to treat the snakes accordingly. Check all wild-collected snakes for parasites through a fecal exam and treat them as needed.

Respiratory Infections

Among the more common diseases of captive snakes are respiratory infections, particularly with tropical snakes kept too cool during the winter months. The signs of respiratory infection include bubbly mucus in and along the sides of the mouth, loss of appetite, inactivity, gaping, and forced exhalations.

In initial stages, usually associated with the presence of bubbly mucus, the first step is to correct the environmental conditions and for most species, to raise the temperature into the 80s F, with a 90° F basking spot. If there are no signs of improvement within a week, or if the snake is demonstrating the gaping, forced exhalation, and extended throat often associated with pneumonia, take it to a qualified veterinarian for treatment. Some viral respiratory infections introduced by wild-collected snakes are easily spread to a collection and can be deadly. The importance of implementing quarantine procedures with any new snake or sick snake cannot be emphasized enough.

Bacterial and Viral Infections

Snakes are subject to a wide range of bacterial and viral infections that manifest as general signs of illness, such as unusual behaviors, weight loss, loss of appetite, inactivity, diarrhea, signs of respiratory infection, refusal to feed, and general weakness. A qualified veterinarian can perform an examination and tests to help identify the problem and hopefully treat the disease. Realize that some viral diseases, such as paramyxovirus and IBD, are infectious and not treatable. Euthanasia of afflicted animals is the best way to prevent the spread of these deadly diseases.

Responsible Snake Ownership

Irresponsible snake owners take their snakes out in public settings, allow their snakes to escape, or mishandle their snakes. By doing these things, they hurt all those who have a serious interest in snakes and keep them responsibly. The following is a set of guidelines for responsible snake ownership:

• Research before you buy. Try to select a species that fills your needs and living conditions. Do not purchase a species that you do not intend to keep long term. Read up on the species' requirements before your purchase.

• Keep snakes in escape-proof, locked enclosures. Escapes are bad publicity and threaten the rights of those who keep snakes responsibly. Snakes can frighten neighbors and, under certain conditions, cause their owner serious and expensive legal liabilities. Snakes have a bad enough reputation without irresponsible owners contributing to it. Buy or build a secure, escape-proof cage.

• Do not display snakes in public. Outside of a proper forum, such as an educational presentation or reptile show, snakes should not be taken into the public. Many people are frightened of snakes and do not relish coming face to face with snakes outside of the proper forums. In several areas of the United States, the display of snakes in public is illegal outside of an appropriate environment.

• Never release unwanted snakes into the wild. There are many outlets for healthy unwanted snakes. Classified ads can be placed in newspapers or on the Internet. You can also offer your snake(s) to pet stores or reptile dealers, and many will offer you a fair distributor or wholesale price. If they won't pay for an unwanted pet snake, they might consider taking it for free. Many herpetological societies have adoption committees that will try to find a home for your unwanted snake. Another recourse is animal shelters; some now accept unwanted snakes. Try a local zoo, veterinary clinic, herpetological society, or local herpetological rescue society. If you still can't find a home for your snake and you must get rid of it in a hurry, have it euthanized by a veterinarian. Under no circumstances should you ever release it.

• Never sell unhealthy snakes. If you no longer want or can no longer take care of a sick snake, have it euthanized. Responsible store owners and hobbyists cannot take a sick snake because of the risks to their existing collections. Although some may consider my view on sick reptiles and amphibians radical, consider the greater good. Better dead than spreading disease and heartache.

Part II:

The Best Display Snakes

INTRODUCTION

Many species of regularly available snakes exhibit the qualities that make good display animals. From a strictly display
standpoint, species that rest in the open or are active during
the day are by far the best, so these are the species that I will
focus on. This section, however, is only an overview with a
focus on vivarium design. For more extensive information
on keeping and breeding specific snake species, consult one
or more of the many good books available in the pet trade.

CHAPTER 17:

PYTHONS

Green Tree Pythons and Carpet Pythons (*Morelia* spp.)

Among the most outstanding display snakes in the world are the members of the genus *Morelia*, which includes carpet pythons, diamond pythons, green tree pythons, Boelen's python, and, the giant of the genus, the amethystine python.

The best display candidates in the genus *Morelia* are arguably green tree pythons *(Morelia viridis)*, which during the day reliably rest in the open, forming an overhanging spiral coil on a horizontally positioned branch. As babies, green tree pythons are one of the most beautiful snakes, colored brilliant yellow, orange, or red. Adults are variable and, depending on their origins, range from solid green, to green and yellow blotched, to mostly yellow. Other forms have a turquoise blue pattern or, more rarely, are completely

Green tree pythons *(Morelia viridis)* were originally imported from Indonesia, but most of the animals now sold in the trade are captive-bred. They generally fare well in naturalistic tropical forest vivaria.

aqua blue. Because of their moderate size, typically between 4 and 5 feet, several individuals can be kept together as long as only a single male is included. Males can inflict deep, damaging lacerations on each other during the breeding season and should not be housed together. A large display with a pair or trio of these snakes is always an eye catcher.

Carpet pythons *(M. spilota)* are semiarboreal, often spending extended periods of time coiled at the fork of branches or on raised shelves. Large forms of the carpet python, such as the coastal carpet python *(M. spilota mcdowelli)*, can exceed 9 feet and are almost too big for anything but a closet- or room-sized enclosure. More suitable are smaller forms, such as jungle carpet pythons *(M. spilota cheynei)*, jungle carpet x diamond python hybrids, and Irian Jaya carpet pythons *(M. spilota* sp.), which typically level off in the 5 to 6 foot range. Of these, carpet x diamond python hybrids and outstanding velvet black and yellow specimens of the jungle carpet python, like those pictured on the cover of David and Tracy Barker's book, *Pythons of the World* (1994), are probably the most strikingly beautiful.

Selection

Captive-bred green tree pythons that are at least 2 feet long are generally hardy and easy-to-maintain captives, feeding

Baby green tree pythons are arguably the most beautiful snakes in the world. However, they can be problem feeders initially, preferring live, active prey such as small lizards or frogs, to baby mice. They also require high humidity and regular misting.

readily with simple requirements. Babies, on the other hand, can be difficult to get started on pink mice and are generally more delicate, more sensitive to errors in husbandry, and best left to more experienced herpetoculturists. Given a choice, it is well worth your while to start with animals that are well established and growing out of the bright red or yellow juvenile coloration.

Carpet pythons are generally hardy at all sizes. Baby carpet pythons have dull coloration and are more nippy than adults. It takes about two years for a young carpet python to fully develop its adult coloration.

Handling

Green tree pythons vary in temperament but most become tame, although there is always a risk of a bite when initially picking them up from a resting position. Like all *Morelia*, hungry green tree pythons may strike at a source of movement. Carpet pythons show some variation in docility between subspecies, although a general pattern is for them to be nippy when young and to grow less prone to biting by the time they reach adult size, as long as they receive regular handling. Of these arboreal pythons, those most likely to remain biters are jungle carpet pythons. Although not as colorful as jungle carpets, Irian Jaya carpet pythons are often tame, even wild-collected adults. Nonetheless, carpet pythons are not a predictably tame species and you should use some caution when handling them. Feeding-conditioned strikes are common when these snakes are hungry. Use a snake stick to initially lift a snake off its perch prior to handling.

Vivarium Design

It is important for both green tree pythons and carpet pythons to have a tall cage, preferably front opening and landscaped with accessible horizontal branches. With green tree pythons the horizontal perches should have a diameter between 50 percent and 100 percent of the mid-body width of the snake maintained. Provide larger horizontal trunks, branch forks, or raised shelves for carpet pythons, because they tend to coil or stretch on top of broader surfaces one or more times their body diameter.

The BSS method works very well with these species and can help provide the relative humidity (minimum 70 percent) they require. In addition, lightly mist each night. Provide these snakes with the proper heat range with basking lights and subtank heating. Ideal daytime temperatures are in the mid 80s F, with a basking spot that reaches 90° F.

Nighttime temperatures should be in the upper 70s F. Failure to provide the proper temperature can result in respiratory and bacterial infections, as well as kidney disease. You can use red lights or ceramic infrared heat lamps at night.

Feeding

When young, offer these snakes live food in the form of pink or fuzzy mice, up to twice the midbody girth of the snake. The prey food should be somewhat larger than what you would think appropriate. Some baby green tree pythons do not feed readily on pink mice and may require many attempts over several weeks before they take food on their own. Some require teasing with the prekilled prey item using forceps. Others feed if offered a live pink mouse while being held in a small container with a perch. With stubborn individuals, try offering a small lizard, such as an anole. Established adults readily feed on live or freshly-killed mice or young rats offered from feeding tongs. During the winter, which corresponds with the breeding season, fasting for varying periods of time is normal. Males may fast for up to five months a year.

Breeding

Green tree and carpet pythons are now bred in significant numbers by hobbyists and commercial breeders. Reduce their photoperiod and lower their temperature 5 to 7 degrees in late fall (November in northern hemisphere) until late winter/early spring. During this cool period introduce the male at weekly or biweekly intervals to the female's enclosure for three days at a time, then remove him. Leave the pair together if you observe copulation.

Provide egg-laying boxes, with moist sphagnum moss, for females to lay their eggs. Depending on the species and incubation conditions, the eggs will hatch in forty-five to sixty days. The high demand for green tree pythons and attractive forms of the carpet python warrants efforts to breed them.

Related Species

Diamond Python *(Morelia spilota spilota)*

One of the most beautiful snakes in the world is the Australian diamond python, characterized by a complex background of dark scales with a light yellowish center and patterned with high-contrast white rosettes outlined in black. Adult size is typically between 5 feet for males and 7 feet for females. The largest specimen on record was a female longer than 10 feet (Barker and Barker, 1994).

Diamond pythons can be displayed like carpet pythons. They are usually arboreal when young, but become more terrestrial after they reach adult size. However, their behaviors in relation to perches depends more on cage design then on an innate tendency. If provided with the right temperature gradients, even large diamond pythons will perch on broad branches or rest on shelves. What sets diamond pythons apart from most other *Morelia* are their temperature requirements. They have adapted to a habitat with extended cool winters and do not fare well if maintained as a tropical snake. During nine months of the year, their cage should have a vertical temperature gradient with basking sites of 84-87° F and a floor area in the upper 70s F. During the winter, cool young diamond pythons into the low to mid 70s F and do not feed them for two to three months. Cool adult diamond pythons like colubrids—in dark containers kept in the 50s and 60s F for three months a year. This is best for their health and conditions them for breeding. Diamond pythons will become sick and die young if kept warm year round and power-fed. They should be grown slowly on an extended feeding regime of one meal every two (babies) to three (adults) weeks. If raised from babies in the right manner, they require up to five years to reach sexual maturity.

Maintain adult diamond pythons on a regime of ten to fifteen meals a year over a period of six to eight months. They should spend three and one-half months fasting during the winter shutdown and another couple of months fasting during the breeding season. See the excellent article by Stan Chiras in *Reptiles* (2000) for more information on keeping and breeding this outstanding species.

Ball Python *(Python regius)*

Attractive appearance, stout proportions, ideal size (between 4 and 6 feet), slow movements, and docility all

The ball python *(Python regius)* is one of the most popular of all snake species. Because it is primarily active at night, it has limited value for a vivarium display.

contribute to the reputation of ball pythons as great pet snakes. Unfortunately, they are not the best display snakes. Given the opportunity, they are nocturnal and will spend most of the day concealed in some kind of shelter. Special attention to design can, however, help display ball pythons in a decorative naturalistic vivarium, allowing you to view them inside shelters or prowling about at night.

Selection

If possible, start with young ball pythons that are 2 feet or less in length. It is a challenge to acclimate imported adults to captivity so they are best left to specialists. Young ball pythons are most likely to acclimate to conditions that allow for some degree of display.

Handling

Most ball pythons are tame and slow moving when in hand, although every once in a while one will feel threatened and suddenly strike and bite. Unfortunately, because of the low cost of imports and their docile demeanor, ball pythons are among the most mistreated of pet snakes. Hundreds, possibly thousands, are purchased each year by inexperienced owners who handle their pets to death.

These secretive snakes are usually so stressed from constant handling that they refuse to feed and eventually develop a syndrome characterized by muscular weakness and limpness. At most, ball pythons should be handled briefly—ten minutes or less—once or twice a week. The constant slithering between the hands that most snakes, including ball pythons, perform during handling is not a sign of contentment but of stress.

Vivarium Design

Potting soils, as well as BSS substrates with a dry surface, work well with ball pythons. Shrublike plants can be included in the setup, as well as sections of wood and large cork-bark shelters. Most ball pythons will choose to spend the day inside a ground-level shelter or, if provided with a mound that is a mix of soil and leaf or grass litter, will

The ball python is selectively bred for attractive pattern and color. This is a piebald ball python, one of the most sought after and expensive morphs.

burrow into the soft mound. To allow for visibility during the day, provide a large open-sided shelter. Some owners have success using lateral shelters, such as sectioned cork rounds placed vertically and anchored securely. Vertically growing small trees, such as umbrella plants, ficus, and dracaena, can be used as decorative background plants. Starting in the early evening, even if the lights are still on, ball pythons will emerge from their shelters. If hungry, they will hunt and may even climb on branches close to the ground. Red lights make observation of their nocturnal activity possible. Keep daytime temperatures in the 80s F and nighttime temperatures in the upper 70s to low 80s F. Provide a basking spot with temperatures reaching 90° F.

Feeding

Young ball pythons and captive-raised adults readily feed on mice, both live and freshly killed. Imported adults can take months, sometimes more than a year, to begin feeding on mice or small rats. For imported adult ball pythons, consult a book specializing in ball pythons. (See References for suggested literature.) If kept in groups, remove ball pythons from the cage and feed them individually in plastic storage containers.

Breeding

Ball pythons will readily breed in captivity if kept with a group of several males and females in large cages and exposed to a period of slight cooling in the winter.

The Children's python *(Antaresia childreni)* is a dwarf Australian python suitable for desert vivaria.

Children's and Spotted Pythons (*Antaresia childreni* and *Antaresia maculosa*)

Children's pythons and spotted pythons are dwarf nocturnal pythons from Australia that can be displayed in desert vivaria. Their small adult size, 3 to 4 feet for spotted pythons and 2½ to 3 feet for Children's pythons, make them particularly appealing for those who want to keep a python but have a limited amount of space. Although they tend to remain concealed during the day, open-front shelters allow for viewing and a red light makes it possible to observe nocturnal activity.

The spotted python *(Antaresia maculosa)* is the most readily available of the dwarf Australian pythons.

Selection

These dwarf pythons are regularly available as captive-bred animals and are typically healthy and hardy at all ages. Some babies may initially be reluctant to feed on mice but perseverance, and as a last resort scenting a pink mouse with a lizard, will get them started.

Handling
Children's pythons are generally docile snakes, but spotted pythons can vary in temperament. Some spotted pythons are nearly impossible to handle without getting bitten.

Vivarium Design
These snakes are found in desert to woodland areas and generally prefer relatively dry vivaria. They fare well on a sandy BSS substrate with rock and wood for decoration. Open-front shelters allow viewing during the day. Because of their small size, include a wide range of arid-adapted plants in their setups, leaving about two-thirds of the floor area open. Use a secondary heat source, such as a ceramic infrared heat bulb or red incandescent bulb, to provide heat at night.

Feeding
These snakes readily feed on mice at all sizes. The few babies reluctant to initially take pink mice can be easily tricked by scenting the mice with a lizard.

Breeding
Kept in pairs, they breed readily if exposed to a reduced photoperiod and a 5 to 7 degree F reduction in the temperature range. Breeding occurs during this cool period and eggs are laid in the spring. Incubate them in perlite or vermiculite kept barely moist, about two parts water to three parts incubating medium by weight (2:3). I have also experimented with allowing spotted pythons to brood their eggs with mixed results—up to 50 percent of the eggs failed to hatch. To provide the right conditions for a female to brood, you need a shelter to allow relative humidity from the underlying substrate to accumulate. The temperature must remain between 86° and 88° F inside the shelter. The female will stay coiled around the clutch and will not feed for the entire period. Incubation time is about fifty days.

CHAPTER 18:

BOAS

Boa Constrictors *(Boa constrictor)*

After more than thirty years in the hobby, boa constrictors still rank as my all-time favorite large snakes. They are attractive, heavy-bodied, and slow-moving snakes. When captive-raised, they tend to be tame. Aesthetically, they have many appealing features, including fine scalation and subtle pastel shades of color, against which the tail—boldly patterned with bright colors—provides a dramatic contrast. The face of boa constrictors also has a special appeal with its somewhat canine proportions; it is characterized by a broad base and elongated snout. With seven or more subspecies (the taxonomy is in need of review and updating) and many population morphs, boa constrictors come in a range of aesthetic flavors. The most beautiful boa constrictors are true red-tailed boas *(Boa constrictor constrictor)*, which, as the name suggests, have tails with bright red blotches interspersed with cream yellow.

This adult Colombian common boa constrictor *(Boa constrictor imperator)* lives in a large naturalistic display. Room-sized enclosures may be impractical for most keepers of these large snakes.

Beware of Inclusion Body Disease

According to some veterinary experts, a significant percentage of captive boa constrictors may be infected with a retrovirus that causes inclusion body disease (IBD), an AIDSlike disease that affects certain boas and pythons and possibly other snake species. Boa constrictors can live for years without showing signs of the disease, so quarantine is not of much use for detection. A liver biopsy, a costly procedure at $175 to $300, is the only reliable way to diagnose IBD. One strain of IBD shows inclusion bodies in the blood and can sometimes be detected in advanced infections, by microscopic examination of a blood smear. Currently, IBD is a potential risk for any captive-bred boa constrictor unless a breeder makes an effort to keep his colony IBD free (testing, euthanizing infected animals, avoiding new additions, and keeping the colony mite-free).

Selection

Under normal circumstances, it is best to buy captive-bred boa constrictors rather than imports because there is a greater chance of their being healthy. Right now buying captive-bred boa constrictors is like playing IBD roulette because a significant number of captive-bred boa constrictors may be infected with this viral disease. Buying a recently imported specimen may be less of an IBD risk

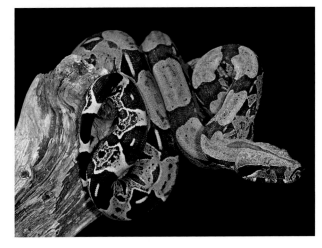

The juvenile red-tailed boa constrictor *(Boa constrictor constrictor)* is a large, attractive South American species. It tends to be nervous in captivity and more prone to biting than Colombian common boas.

159

than a randomly purchased captive-bred specimen. If you're serious about boa constrictors and want to keep one long term, try to find breeders who are working on establishing IBD-free colonies. You may end up paying more for babies, but the extra expense will be well worth it in the long run.

Vivarium Design

Most boa constrictor subspecies and morphs grow large, so adults do best in enclosures at least 6 feet long and 2 feet wide. Ideally, a display should have a height of at least half the length of the snake so that there is room for arboreal perches or shelves. Babies of most forms are arboreal and readily perch on dry branches or in larger plants. Larger boas tend to spend most of their time on the ground, on tree trunks angled across a cage, or on raised shelves.

Potting soil or BSS substrate generally works well with boa constrictors, as long as fecal mass, which can be substantial in adult specimens, is removed. In standard cage design, place tall plants or trees toward the back of the enclosure. In front, use firmly anchored tree branches with section diameters equal to twice the width of the snake's body. Tree trunks, large branches, and hollow logs can also be placed at the base of the enclosure as access areas and shelters. Scantily plant the ground with medium-sized shrubs. Except for babies up to about 3 feet in length, use plants for their decorative effect and not as perching areas. Hollow logs or sectioned tree trunks of the appropriate size are the most natural looking shelters for boa constrictors.

Handling

In terms of handling and tameness there is a great range in the various boa subspecies and forms. The most consistently tame boa constrictors are the common boas *(B. constrictor imperator)* originally imported from Colombia. As a rule, red-tailed boas *(B. c. constrictor)* are more prone to striking and biting. Many boa constrictors also undergo a positive behavioral change; they are nasty and hissing when young but calm and tame by the time they reach sexual maturity. This pattern is typical with Argentine boa constrictors *(B. constrictor occidentalis)*. An exception is the popular Colombian common boa, which tends to be docile at all ages.

If hungry or frightened, even the tamest boa constrictor is capable of a sudden and unexpected strike. Reading the body language of a boa constrictor, such as an S coil in the front part of the body and a partially raised or fully raised head, allows you to predict the risk of a bite. As a rule, regular handling starting when the snake is young results in tamer individuals. Still, caution is warranted if a boa is hungry and has not been handled for some time. I have received several reports of boa constrictor bites by owners surprised that their tame specimen would strike at them.

Bites by larger boa constrictors are painful and can result in multiple lacerations and bruising. More rarely, bites by large boas can cause wounds that require stitches. Fortunately, boa bites are usually quick bite-release incidents and seldom of serious consequence. There is no record of a human fatality by a boa constrictor. In one case, notable because of the seriousness of the injury, an owner was bitten in the eye by a young red-tailed boa. Some caution is warranted prior to and during the handling of larger boa constrictors.

Feeding

Boa constrictors readily feed on prekilled rodents of the appropriate size (girth of prey half to equal the midbody girth of the snake). Start boa constrictors on small, fuzzy mice when young and switch them to small rats as they approach 4 feet in length. The size and number of prey items per feeding, frequency of feeding, and ambient temperature determines the growth rate and the final size of captive boas. Under controlled feeding regimes, Colombian boa constrictors can exceed 9 feet in length and red-tailed boa constrictors can reach 11 feet in length. Under a more restricted feeding regime, offering a single moderate-size prey item every two to three weeks, both subspecies will level off between 5 and 8 feet in length.

Dwarf forms of the Central American common boa constrictors, such as Hog Island, Craw Cay, and Corn Island boas, can be stunted at a length under 5 feet if fed only every three weeks. In contrast, boa constrictors kept warm and under an intensive feeding regime grow fast and breed young. If adults are kept long-term on an intensive, weekly feeding of one or more large prey items, they develop signs of grotesque obesity—looking like stuffed sausages with skin creases and lumpy sides.

Breeding

Boa constrictors are live-bearing and breed readily in captivity, particularly Colombian common boas. Various procedures, including group breeding, multiple males per female, and single pairings, have been successful. Breeding typically occurs in the fall or winter when the temperature is lowered 5 to 10 degrees (this can vary depending on sub-species), the photoperiod is reduced, and the animals are not fed. See the excellent chapter by Jeff Ronne in the *Boa Constrictor Manual* (1998) for details on breeding procedures.

Provide gravid females a hot spot (around 95° F) large enough to coil upon. Boa constrictors, depending on their size and physical condition, will give birth to up to sixty young. Because there must be a concerted effort to reduce the spread of IBD and cull IBD-infected boas, developing IBD-free breeding colonies of all boa constrictors deserves urgent attention. IBD-infected boas should be euthanized unless they are kept as single pets. They should never be sold, given away, or mixed with other snakes.

Related Species

Dumeril's Boa *(Acrantophis dumerili)*
Dumeril's boa hails from the island of Madagascar and is so closely related to boa constrictors that its inclusion in the same genus has been proposed (Kluge, 1991).

An attractive color and pattern, comfortable adult size (between 4 and 5 feet), and a generally docile temperament make this species a hobbyists' favorite. These snakes prefer

Dumeril's boas *(Acrantophis dumerili)* are Madagascar's version of boa constrictors. They can be kept on a sandy, dry surface substrate with cork bark rounds as shelters. Use trees in the background, with thick branches placed at an angle for the snakes to climb.

drier conditions than boa constrictors and are primarily terrestrial. Although they may use shelves, they seldom coil on branches. Use hollow logs as shelters.

The Dumeril's boa is listed as endangered under Appendix I of the Convention on International Trade in Endangered Species (CITES), meaning it is threatened, so there are few exports and captive stock is inbred or closely related because of the small number of foundation stock. Defects associated with inbreeding have been reported in captive animals.

Like boa constrictors, Dumeril's boas give birth to live young, with litters of up to twenty on record.

Emerald Tree Boa *(Corallus caninus)*

Emerald tree boas are similar in general appearance and habits to green tree pythons. They rank among the most impressive display snakes in the world and can generally be kept in the same manner as green tree pythons, except that they require a lower temperature range.

Several morphs of emerald tree boas are recognized, including a typical green and white morph, a patternless green morph, and a dark green "black" morph. The most beautiful and docile of the emerald tree boas is the Amazon Basin morph. Some specialists argue that Amazon Basin emeralds are different enough in head scalation, potential size, and pattern to deserve subspecies status. Outstanding specimens of Amazon Basin emeralds are also characterized by a more or less solid white mid-dorsal

The emerald tree boa *(Corallus caninus)* is one of the most beautiful of the snakes. Its arboreal perching habits make it one of the best selections for an attractive tropical forest display. Provide high humidity through daily misting and keep daytime temperatures in the mid 80s.

stripe. As a warning, for their size, emerald tree boas have the largest teeth of any nonvenomous snake.

Selection

Young animals in the 2-foot range are probably the best to start with. Large wild-caught adults require experience to establish and babies—both imported and captive bred—can be delicate.

Vivarium Design

Use tall enclosures with horizontal branches and perches sized 50 to 70 percent of the midbody girth of your snakes. Place a basking light over an open area of the tallest perch. Use plants, such as dracaenas and umbrella plants, as background and access rather than as perching sites. Relative humidity of at least 70 percent is important for this species and should be provided through live plants in pots, a moist substrate, and a single nightly misting. When a snake is in

Juvenile emerald tree boas start off bright orange and gradually shift to green with bright white dorsal blotches.

shed, increase misting to twice a day. Include ground-level plants for decorative purposes. The air temperature of the enclosure should be between 78° F and 83° F at the cool end of the enclosure, with a basking site reaching 90° F at the other end. The temperature can drop by 5 degrees at night.

Feeding

Emerald tree boas are not overly active snakes and fare best if fed a single, appropriately sized prey item every two to three weeks. Overfeeding and being kept at too high a temperature can lead to regurgitation or obesity. Emerald tree boas often only accept warm prey, so it's best to feed them fresh-killed mice or rats. If previously frozen, the prey must be thawed and heated (up to 100° F). Offer food with forceps or feeding tongs, depending on the snake's size. Some individuals, particularly imports, require live prey (preferably young rats) to start feeding. A small percentage of imports may initially feed only on birds, such as live chicks.

Provide this species with a large water container and mist nightly to raise the tank humidity. Emerald tree boas will also drink from mist-formed water drops.

Handling

Emerald tree boas generally should not be handled, although some individuals, particularly Amazon Basin emeralds, can become relatively tame if handled regularly from a young age. Use a snake hook to initially guide an emerald tree boa from a sleeping position onto a hand. Always keep the head away from your face. If you want a handleable emerald tree boa, it is best to start with a young animal. Only handle tree boas during the day, as they are more prone to biting at night. Having been struck by a nasty, wild-caught 5½-foot female emerald tree boa that left a tooth embedded in my thumb, trust me when I tell you that this is not a species you want biting you. Use caution.

Breeding

A 5 to 7 degree drop in temperature range starting in November, combined with regular nightly misting, often results in breeding activity sometime between December and June. Keep animals in pairs or introduce a male into a female's enclosure at weekly to biweekly intervals to prompt breeding. The gestation period can range from seven to nine months depending on environmental conditions. Provide a warm basking spot between 90° F and 95° F for gravid females and offer smaller sized prey (half the midbody girth) during the gestation period.

Related Species

Amazon tree boas *(Corallus hortulanus)* are regularly available and can be kept under the same conditions as emerald tree boas. These are less heavy-bodied than emerald tree boas and tend to be semiarboreal. They do not typically form the overhanging spiral coil of emerald tree boas but rather a loose coil on the ground, on a raised basking site, in foliage, or at a branch fork. Although the typical brownish forms are not particularly attractive, this species is polychromatic and also comes in reds, oranges, yellows, and an interesting combination of silvery white and purplish brown known as the garden tree boa.

The most negative feature of Amazon tree boas is their propensity to readily strike from a great distance, inflicting painful skin-puncturing bites with their long teeth. They rank among the most aggressive of nonvenomous snakes. If raised from babies (when the bites are less painful and damaging) and handled regularly, you are likely to be among the few to have a semitame Amazon tree boa. For obvious reasons, caution is required when handling or performing maintenance with this species. Their tendency

Shown is an outstanding example of a red-phase Amazon tree boa.

to bite also makes them best kept singly, unless you have a very large cage.

Many Amazon tree boas tend to hide or stay at ground level during the day, unless they can find raised resting areas with overhead shelters such as the dense foliage from a tree. Eliminating or limiting ground-level shelters create conditions that cause these snakes to select more prominent daytime perching areas. As with other *Corallus*, this species sleeps during the day and is mostly active at night. Subadult and adult Amazon tree boas readily feed on mice of the appropriate size. Because lizards are their preferred food, babies sometimes need a little coaxing to start feeding on pink mice. Several specialized breeders offer attractive yellow or orange red forms of this species. It is also still imported in small numbers from Suriname and Guyana.

Brazilian Rainbow Boas
(Epicrates cenchria)

In recent years, captive breeding has allowed regular availability of the Brazilian rainbow boa, one of the most beautiful snakes in the world. Brazilian rainbow boas are characterized by an easily manageable size, vivid orange red

The Brazilian rainbow boa (Epicrates cenchria) is a nocturnal species best displayed in low light and plant cover.

to purplish brown background coloration, and round mid-dorsal blotches. Like other snakes with mid-dorsal blotches, rainbow boas are primarily terrestrial. The purpose of the pattern is probably to disrupt the visual unity of the body form, preventing predation by birds that hunt by sight. This species was given the common name of rainbow boa because of the high degree of iridescence generated by its smooth scales when exposed to sunlight. Iridescence is a feature found in several snake species that live in humid environments including moist substrates or leaf litter.

Selection
Relatively few rainbow boas are currently imported. Most are captive bred, healthy, and easy to raise. The most popular and readily available are the orange red Amazonian rainbow boas *(Epicrates cenchria cenchria)*, which are typically sold under the name of Brazilian rainbow boas.

Vivarium Design
Rainbow boas are primarily terrestrial and nocturnal. They fare well if kept on a moist substrate, including potting soils and BSS substrates. Moist substrates help provide the higher relative humidity (around 80 percent) this species requires. Apply the BSS method to Brazilian rainbow boa enclosures by combining a deep, sandy BSS substrate layer with a depressed area to allow for watering from the bottom up. A layer of leaf litter or cypress mulch on top of the substrate gives the display a more natural appearance.

Setup design plays a key role in the display potential of the species. Live plants, with enough canopy to provide shade and lateral or open-front shelters provide the security necessary for this species to rest in the open, rather than spend all of its time concealed in a shelter. The vivarium should be mostly shaded by plant canopy or a shelf, with only a small exposed area beneath a basking site. Use a sub-tank heater to provide the consistent warm temperatures this species prefers. The temperature at ground level should be around 80° F, with a basking site of 90-95° F. At night, the temperature can drop by up to 5 degrees.

Feeding

Rainbow boas readily feed on mice of the appropriate size at all ages. Larger specimens will take small rats.

Handling

Although juvenile and imported rainbow boas are initially nippy, most eventually become tame and are easily handled.

Breeding

A winter drop of 5 to 7 degrees, a reduced photoperiod, and fasting between November and February provide the conditions for breeding. During this period, and up through March, introduce males at regular intervals into the females' enclosures or keep the animals in pairs. Gravid females should have a hot spot of 90-95° F. Gestation lasts about six months, but depending on conditions can range from four to eight months.

Rosy Boas *(Lichanura trivirgata)*

Rosy boas are one of two boa species found in the United States. Their moderate size—around 3 feet—combined with a natural tameness make them popular snake pets. When displayed under LAM conditions, they tend to be rather dull snakes, but they have great qualities for the art of keeping snakes. They're attractive, slow moving, and easy to maintain. Much to my surprise, rosy boas turned

The California rosy boa *(Lichanura trivirgata)* is related to the sand boas. It is a hardy and easy-to-keep captive that displays well in a desert vivarium.

out a to be a good display species. They do not mind being partially exposed and are active at different times during the day. The individuals I tested also readily perched on wood and sturdy plants. Various subspecies and several morphs, including a couple of albino forms, are now bred in good numbers and are readily available in the pet trade. This species is a good choice for desert vivaria.

Vivarium Design

Minimum vivarium size for adults is at least 36 inches long. A dry, sandy substrate, which is all sand or a sand, soil, and peat mix, works well. As with Brazilian rainbow boas, create a depressed area or hollow in the substrate, then slowly pour water in the depression to moisten the substrate from the bottom up and keep the surface dry. Include overhead basking heat lamps to produce relatively quick surface drying. Landscape the vivarium with wood or stacked rock, forming shelters at the ground level. Position lights over rock or wood stumps to entice rosy boas to bask during the day. Open-front shelters allow viewing during the day. Rosy boas will also rest in lateral shelters, such as between landscape structures and the sides of an enclosure.

Rosy boas drink little and require only a small water container. Wet or humid conditions and poor ventilation can result in skin and respiratory diseases.

Handling

Rosy boas have the reputation of being tame and are considered among the best of pet snakes. However, some individuals—much to the surprise of their owners—strike and bite readily.

Feeding

Once established, rosy boas are aggressive feeders. When hungry they may strike quickly at an approaching hand. Adults and babies readily take mice of the appropriate size, although some babies can take a while to start feeding. Rosy boas will also stop feeding intermittently. Starting in late fall or early winter, they will typically fast for up to four months and then resume feeding in late winter or early spring.

Breeding

This species is now bred in good numbers by hobbyists. A period of winter cooling and reduced photoperiod conditions this species to breed and breeding occurs in late spring. Like other boas, the rosy boa gives birth to live young, between five and ten per litter. The record is twelve.

Several morphs of rosy boas are now bred in captivity. Small size and docility have made this species increasingly popular.

Pacific Boas (*Candoia spp.*)

The Pacific boas include the Solomon Islands ground boa (*Candoia carinata paulsoni*), Solomon Islands tree boa (*Candoia bibroni australis*), Indonesian dwarf boa

Solomon Island ground boas *(Candoia carinata paulsoni)* are secretive and usually remain concealed in a shelter during the day.

172

(Candoia carinata carinata), Indonesian tree boa *(Candoia bibroni bibroni)*, and the viper boa *(Candoia aspera)*.

Pacific boas are odd creatures with stout proportions and a subtle aesthetic beauty, consisting of long faces, complex patterning, and a wide range of color and patterns, which make them very appealing displays in the right kind of setup. Their heavy body, triangular head, and vertical pupils give them the appearance of a venomous ground viper. With the exception of the thick-bodied viper boa, they come in a variety of colors and patterns, including beautiful combinations of pastel shades of whitish to pinkish tans contrasting with rich orange brown patterns. Others can be reddish orange or brownish yellow with an iridescent sheen. Pacific boas are probably the most polychromatic (showing great variation in color) boas available.

Pacific boas are currently imported from two areas. The Solomon Islands export the large, very attractive, and very variable Solomon Islands ground boa *(Candoia carinata paulsoni)* and the Solomon Islands tree boa *(C. bibroni australis)*. Indonesia exports small numbers of the Indonesian dwarf boa *(C. c. carinata)*, the Pacific tree boa *(C. bibroni bibroni)*, and the short, squat viper boa *(C. aspera)*, one of the most heavy-bodied of the nonvenomous snakes.

Selection

The great majority of Pacific boas offered for sale are imported, although captive-born babies from imported females and, more rarely, captive-bred babies are available at various times. The few captive-bred Pacific boas are colorful morphs. The most popular is the pale San Isabel Island morph of the Solomon Islands ground boa, which has a cream white background and a high-contrast reddish pattern. Compared to other imported snakes, most Pacific boas arrive in reasonably good condition and many establish well in captivity under the proper conditions. Babies are generally difficult to start feeding, preferring live small lizards or frogs. Purchase larger specimens if you want to avoid the hassle of starting babies on mice.

Solomon Islands ground boas are primarily terrestrial, although they will climb onto shelves or into shelters raised a short distance from the ground. They do well on a BSS substrate if the surface is allowed to dry. Relative humidity should be around 70 percent. An open-front shelter, such as a cork log placed on its side, allows viewing during the day. The temperature should range between 78° and 84° F. Some specimens, even if in shelters, will expose parts of their body to an area heated by an overhead bulb to thermoregulate.

Indonesian dwarf Pacific boas *(C. carinata carinata)* are so unlike the Solomon Islands ground boas that they will one day be recognized as a separate species. They are small, slender-bodied, and semiarboreal snakes. Because of their small size (under 2 feet) they can be kept in small enclosures. They make poor display snakes because they are secretive and strictly nocturnal, and prefer feeding on frogs or small lizards. In my setups, they spent most of the day concealed under cork bark or hidden between foliage of birds nest fern and bromeliads. Like other Pacific boas, they are active at night and can be viewed under low-wattage incandescent red lights.

Pacific tree boas *(C. bibroni)* are semiarboreal and can be maintained in vivaria designed as for carpet pythons but with larger branches for perching. These snakes will rest in ground-level or raised shelters during the day but are active in branches at night. Certain rosette-forming plants with stacks of overlapping leaves, such as birds nest ferns, bromeliads, and dracaenas, provide natural shelters for smaller specimens. Provide branches with overhanging foliage as security for these snakes to lie in the open during the day. Mist nightly. The temperature should be in the low to mid-80s during the day, dropping 5 to 7° F at night. Provide an overhead basking light during the day.

Viper boas are squat, nocturnal ground dwellers that like high relative humidity and moist moss or leaf litter covering a section of the floor of the enclosure. Their appearance is said to mimic the death adder. If provided with an open-front shelter, viper boas display comparatively

Pacific tree boas *(Candoia bibroni)* are semiarboreal and, like Amazon tree boas, will perch on above-ground branches or in open tree hollows if the overhead foliage provides enough security.

well. Use various low-light plants for decoration. Provide a consistently warm ground temperature, between 78° F and 82° F, during the day, with an overhead basking light at the edge of a shaded area. A large, shallow water container must be available at all times.

Feeding

With the exception of Indonesian dwarf Pacific boas, which prefer small frogs at all ages, most subadult and adult Pacific boas feed readily on mice. Baby Pacific boas start off feeding on lizards or frogs and can be problematic to start on pink mice. Baby Indonesian dwarf Pacific boas are so tiny that they require small, newly metamorphosed frogs. A high level of prey activity is important to elicit striking. Babies will strike and feed on live fish such as guppies that are allowed to flip around on dry land, but I haven't had long-term success raising babies on a fish-only diet.

Solomon Island boas and Pacific tree boas are the most likely to begin feeding on newborn live mice, although it can take weeks and many feeding attempts before they finally capture and eat the prey. Scenting pinkies with house geckos or green tree frogs will sometimes convince reluctant feeders to start eating.

Handling

Pacific boas are easily handled and most will not readily bite, but they are shy and simple-minded as far as snakes go, showing few signs of responsiveness. Occasionally, you'll observe a normally tame Pacific boa perform sudden quick strike-and-bite sequences because it interpreted something about the situation as threatening. Some individuals, notably viper boas, are more prone to striking and biting. As can be expected, the bites are painful but of little consequence aside from tiny multiple punctures and small lacerations.

Breeding

Few breeders work with Pacific boas because they appeal mostly to a specialist market and the price of imports doesn't justify the cost and effort to breed them. However, they can be quite prolific and reduced availability of imports in recent years suggests greater efforts should be made at captive propagation. Among the tricks to breeding these boas is a cooling period of up to six weeks, consisting of a nightly drop into the upper 60s F, with daytime temperatures climbing to within normal range, around 80° F. The other breeding secret is to use multiple males. As with other boas, Pacific boas are live bearing.

CHAPTER 19:

WATER SNAKES AND GARTER SNAKES

These snakes typically live near freshwater sources, along the edges of ponds, streams, and rivers. They are nonconstricting predators and feed primarily on fish and amphibians.

Water Snakes (Genus *Nerodia, Natrix, Enhydris*)

For years, water snakes, which live near water and feed on aquatic organisms, were considered cheap snakes with undesirable characteristics. Although not recommended

The red mangrove water snake *(Nerodia clarkii compressicauda)* is a Florida species that is usually found near brackish water. The attractive red phase is of particular interest to hobbyists.

for those interested in a handleable pet, many water snakes have outstanding display potential and easy care requirements. They are often active during the day and spend extended periods of time basking in the open or soaking and swimming in water. For those who want to own a snake but are unwilling to feed it rodents, water snakes have the added advantage of readily feeding on fish—live, frozen and thawed, or cut fillet sections coated with a vitamin/mineral supplement.

Contrary to what many think, some water snakes are attractive. Among the most beautiful are the red and orange forms of the mangrove water snake *(Nerodia clarkii compressicauda)*, red-bellied water snakes *(N. erythrogaster)*, and high red forms of the Florida banded water snake *(N. fasciata)*. Rarely available, but usually quite beautiful, are albino morphs of water snakes, currently bred in small numbers by only a few individuals. Although many other species exhibit dull coloration, their crisp patterns (such as found in the brown water snakes), unusual form (such as the bunched face of some species), and interesting behaviors all have special appeal. The largest species available to hobbyists is the dull-colored green water snake *(N. cyclopion)*, which is heavy bodied and can reach a length up to 6 feet. As adults, they are only suitable for very large, preferably room-sized vivaria. The nominal subspecies *N. cyclopion cyclopion* is said to be more diurnal and more likely to rest in overhanging trees than the Florida green water snake *(N. cyclopion floridana)*.

Non-native water snakes are also occasionally available from specialist stores and dealers. Although rarely available in the United States, the European species of *Natrix*, such as the viperine and diced water snakes *(N. maura* and *N. tesselata)*, are generally desirable, even if not particularly colorful. Rarely, a few exotic species of water snakes become available. These include some of the rear-fanged Asian and South American species. The leucistic *Enhydris*, white with tiny black eyes, is unusual and attractive. Because they have a potentially fatal bite, avoid Asian water snakes of the genus *Rhabdophis*.

The northern water snake *(Nerodia sipedon sipedon)* is dull colored but displays well and is often active during the day.

Selection

Because they are more likely to adapt to captivity and less likely to be diseased, it is best to start with babies or smaller specimens of water snakes when available. Adults of some wild-caught species, such as brown water snakes and Asian *Enhydrys*, often fail to adapt to captivity and end up dying, whereas younger specimens typically do well in captivity.

Vivarium Design

Depending on the species, there are two approaches to water snake displays. One is to create a sizeable land area over an aquarium, with driftwood sections leading from the water to the land area. The large water area makes this kind of vivarium particularly appealing. Many water snakes bask coiled on raised branches from trees or driftwood sections. The second method is to use a BSS substrate with large water containers such as plastic dog bowls or storage boxes that allow for easy water changes. In my tests, the BSS system works remarkably well with water snakes and results in an odor-free environment as long as the water is replaced regularly and fecal masses scooped out. Some of the most challenging kinds of vivarium design can be accomplished with water snake setups, combining a land section using the BSS system and a water section consisting of a planted aquarium with biological filtration.

I've been asked whether water snakes can be kept with other species; it's challenging, but some combinations are possible. Small water turtles can be included in large water snake displays, as can groups of small fish as long as there is a large volume of water. Larger water snakes generally have less interest in catching small fish and a more difficult time doing so in a large aquarium. The dual land-water system makes for a challenging project but allows for combining a wide range of plants, including shoreline plants and aquatics. The environmental complexity of water snake vivaria is valued by educators, providing teachers with lecture material on ecosystems and the importance of microbial communities.

Note: When siphoning water from water snake setups, always use a manual siphon or water pump. Never start a siphon with the mouth because of the risks of contracting disease.

Handling

Water snakes vary in their docility and reactions to handling. Most are restless and tend to writhe when in hand. They will readily escape and fall to the ground. Their most noxious behavior, however, is their propensity to

Water snakes can be kept on thick cork-bark slabs floating in water. This is a line of albino banded water snakes the author is trying to establish.

excrete a foul-smelling musk when they feel annoyed or threatened in the course of handling. Some may regurgitate when stressed or strike and bite in quick bite release sequences, although some may hold on and chew. Leather gloves are useful for handling nasty water snakes. Most water snakes, particularly if raised from babies, settle down and allow brief periods of handling, although they may have occasional periods of panic reactions accompanied by musking and strikes. Water snakes are probably not a good choice if handling is a priority.

Feeding

Water snakes feed on live or dead feeder fish, tadpoles, frogs, strips of fish fillet dipped in a vitamin/mineral supplement, and fish-scented prekilled mice. In captivity, feed every seven to ten days. Under certain conditions, they can be cannibalistic, feeding on other small water snakes—even their own babies. After picking up the scent of prey, water snakes are attracted to any movement, including other feeding water snakes. In fact, they often seem more attracted to prey in another snake's mouth than the prey right in front of their nose. On more than one occasion, I have pulled a half-swallowed water snake from the mouth of a larger specimen. If you keep multiple water snakes in the same enclosure, feed them separately in individual plastic storage containers.

Some keepers recommend switching them to mice because they claim snakes on a fish-only diet have particularly foul-smelling feces. However, this has not been the case when water snakes are kept using the BSS system. In fact, the BSS system was first developed using fish-eating water snakes as the experimental subjects, with very positive results. The main reason for trying to switch water snakes to fish-scented fuzzy mice is that whole feeder fish can harbor parasites or bacteria harmful to water snakes.

Breeding

If cooled for a couple of months, most temperate water snakes will breed readily in captivity. Subtropical and

Eastern garter snakes *(Thamnophis s. sirtalis)* are popular pets but are usually kept in small, bare tanks. Keep them in larger, planted vivaria with open areas so you can observe them during the day as they bask and search for food.

tropical species breed at any time of the year. Depending on the genus and species, water snakes are either live bearing or egg laying. Water snakes of the genus *Natrix* are egg laying, while the North American water snakes of the genus *Nerodia* and Asian water snakes of the genus *Enhydris* are live bearing. U.S. water snakes will cannibalize their young unless kept well fed, so provide narrow access shelters that cannot be reached by the female. Move babies to a separate enclosure as soon as you notice them.

As a group, water snakes have been neglected by herpetoculturists and deserve more attention as display species. They rank among my favorite display snakes.

Garter Snakes and Ribbon Snakes (Genus *Thamnophis*)

Like water snakes, garter snakes are generally under-appreciated by hobbyists, and for years were assigned low status. In fact, the genus contains several attractive and interesting species, including the spectacular San Francisco garter snake (an endangered species both state and federally protected, garter snakes cannot be owned or bred by the private sector in the United States—they are, however, bred in decent numbers in Europe), red-sided garter snakes, and the spectacular "flame" line of the eastern garter snake, developed by herpetoculturist Philippe Blais in Canada.

Albino checkered garter snakes *(Thamnophis marcianus)* are bred in small numbers by specialized hobbyists.

Several albino morphs and other mutations are also available from specialist breeders. The most readily available, and one of the most attractive, is the albino morph of the checkered garter snake.

Ribbon snakes can be maintained like garter snakes. Because they are active during the day and readily stay out in the open, they make outstanding display snakes for planted vivaria.

Selection

Most garter snakes offered for sale are wild-collected adults. Captive-born or -bred babies are occasionally

The eastern ribbon snake *(Thamnophis sauritus)* is a U.S. species sold in the pet trade. If kept in a large, planted enclosure with open spaces, it is active during the day. It readily feeds on small fish.

available. Compared to many wild-collected snakes, garter snakes fare well in captivity, as long as they are checked and treated for parasites.

Vivarium Design

Garter snakes and ribbon snakes are primarily terrestrial, although some climb low shrubs and rock structures. They enjoy hunting and spending periods of time in open, sparsely planted areas. For this reason, the vivarium surface should consist of at least 50 percent open area. Place taller plants toward the back of the vivarium and shrublike plants in the middle ground. Rocks and wood should also be toward the back or in the middle ground of the tank. Supply a large container of clean water at all times and place a basking light over a flat rock or wood. Hibernation is recommended.

Handling

Unlike water snakes, garter snakes tend to be docile, although they may musk and will readily drop from your hand. Most become tame.

Feeding

Garter snakes will feed on fish; frogs; scented mice; earthworms; prepared foods, such as supplemented fish fillet strips; and commercial diets, such as T-Rex Garter Grub. An obvious advantage of this group is that they don't have to be fed mice and fare reasonably well on vitamin- and mineral-supplemented fresh fish fillets. They can also be trained to feed on prekilled, fish-scented mice of the appropriate size. Baby garter snakes and smaller species, such as Butler's garter snakes, usually feed readily on earthworms. If you feed garter snakes a primarily fish diet, you must heat the fish prior to supplementation to break down the enzyme thiaminase, which is linked to a vitamin deficiency disease.

Like water snakes, garter snakes suffer the stigma of being smelly snakes because of their foul-smelling feces. However, garter snakes are ideal candidates for applying the BSS system; once activated, the substrate is odor free and easy to maintain.

Breeding

Most garter snakes breed readily after a three-month winter cooling period. Southern forms will breed if cooled into the 60s for two to three months during the winter, but northern forms may require a period of cooling down to 50° F to successfully reproduce. Reduce the photoperiod from fourteen hours of light daily to ten hours daily during prebreeding conditioning. Garter snakes and ribbon snakes are live bearers. Depending on the species, size, condition, and age of adult females, litters can range from five to eighty-five young.

Species with Similar Care

The Chinese Aquatic Rat Snake (Elaphe rufodorsata)

This is an odd diurnal Asian rat snake that has adapted to living along bodies of water and feeds on fish and amphibians, just like garter snakes. Its care is similar to that of garter snakes. Interestingly, this rat snake, like North American water snakes and garter snakes and unlike other rat snakes, is a live bearer, with litters of up to twenty young.

CHAPTER 20:

HOGNOSE SNAKES

Moderate size, stout proportions, and an endearing face with an up turned snout have made hognose snakes increasingly popular in recent years. Western hognose *(Heterodon nasicus nasicus)* and Mexican hognose snakes *(H. n. kennerlyi)* are now bred with regularity and rank among the very best pet snakes. Eastern and southern hognose snakes *(H. platyrhinos* and *H. simus)* are generally considered problematic to keep because of their specialization for feeding on toads. However, some keepers have had success switching them to toad-scented, prekilled mice. All hognose species are partially diurnal, coming out in the mornings and late afternoon, and therefore good candidates for the art of keeping snakes.

Selection
Western and Mexican hognose snakes of all sizes generally adapt well to captivity, but you should begin with

The tricolor hognose snake *(Lystrophis semicinctus)* is originally imported from Argentina and Paraguay. It is bred in small numbers and ranks as one of the highest priced colubrid snakes in the reptile market.

established, feeding, captive-bred and -raised animals instead of wild-caught ones because they are less likely to be infected with parasites. High loads of nematodes can be common in wild-caught specimens.

If interested specifically in eastern and southern hognose snakes, a few specialized hobbyists offer babies that are trained to feed on toad-scented pink mice. Adult hognoses can be trained to switch to prekilled, toad-scented mice. In time, some individuals learn to feed on unscented mice. Scattered efforts to establish mouse-feeding captive populations of southern and eastern hognose snakes have been unsuccessful—self-sustaining captive populations of these species are not yet established.

Eastern and southern hognose are such attractive and interesting snakes that they deserve every effort to firmly establish them in the hobby. A potentially high reproductive rate makes the Eastern hognose snake a particularly good candidate for commercial-scale production.

Vivarium Design

In nature, hognose snakes live on sand or gravel substrates. A deep, sandy BSS mix works for these species if the surface is allowed to dry out. An alternative is a dry, sandy soil mix, as long as fecal material is regularly scooped out and the substrate replaced as needed.

Risks of intestinal impaction are often raised when considering sand substrates for a variety of herps, including hognose snakes. This is the kind of generalization that is becoming common with the armies of self-made experts on the Internet. In the wild, snakes that live on sandy substrates don't usually die of impaction. The risk of impaction is always related to special conditions that result in unusually large amounts of sand or gravel being ingested during feeding. Offering food in a shallow dish and mixing soil with small-grade sand will usually reduce the amount of ingested sand to safe levels.

From an aesthetic standpoint, short, grassy plants and shrubs capable of surviving in sandy soils are best. Take care with landscaping because these snakes are burrowers. They use their upturned snout as a shovel to create burrows beneath objects or at the base of plants. It can also be used to push dirt for sealing a burrow opening. In captivity, hognose snakes tend to burrow beneath objects, such as rocks, wood, water dishes, and even the base of plants, risking crush injuries. Heavy landscape structures should rest directly on the tank bottom or on objects that rest on the tank bottom.

Activity patterns of hognose snakes kept in naturalistic vivaria consist of extended periods of time spent buried, often under landscape structures, alternating with periods spent basking, usually in the morning or at the end of the day. When hungry, they are out looking for food. If you want to prevent hognose snakes from spending extended periods of time underground, rest landscape structures directly on the tank bottom and keep the substrate depth around 2 inches. With the BSS system, take care when stirring the substrate because hognose snakes may be buried underground and can be injured by the stirring instrument.

Handling

Hognose snakes have a reputation as excellent pet snakes because they do not usually bite as a defensive behavior. They rank among the most docile of the snakes. However, they are rear-fanged and mildly venomous. In case of an accidental bite, their venom can cause a reaction if prolonged chewing is allowed. There is one case that I personally witnessed when an individual was accidentally bitten in the ankle when hand-feeding a western hognose on the floor of his home. The snake, once it latched on, started chewing as if it had caught its prey. The owner, finding this behavior amusing, let the snake chew for a short time before removing it. Following the bite, the ankle and lower leg swelled up, accompanied by severe pain and discomfort. The bite eventually lead to three days of hospitalization. If you are bitten by a hognose snake, do not allow it to hang on and chew, even if the bite is no initially painful. Remove it immediately.

Feeding

Western and Mexican hognose snakes readily consume prekilled mice of the appropriate size at all ages. Eastern and southern hognose snakes feed primarily on toads and require scenting of prekilled mice with wet toad or spadefoot toad skin if switched to rodent prey.

Breeding

Western and Mexican hognose snakes are now bred with regularity by hobbyists using standard colubrid breeding techniques of winter cooling. Western hognose snakes can lay up to twenty-three eggs. The eastern hognose snake can be very prolific, with clutch sizes ranging from four to sixty-one.

Related Species

Available only in recent years as captive-bred specimens are the little gems originally imported from Argentina and Paraguay known as tri-colored hognose snakes *(Lystrophis semicinctus)*. They have all the appealing features of regular hognose snakes, along with a striking combination of color and pattern, consisting of red, pure black, and cream white bands. Tri-colored hognose snakes can be kept like other hognose snakes. Captive-bred young eventually learn to feed on mice.

CHAPTER 21

RAT SNAKES

R at snake is the general term for snakes in the genus *Elaphe* and related genera. They form a diverse group with forms that are mostly terrestrial and others that are semiarboreal and ideal for display.

Corn Snakes *(Elaphe guttata guttata)*

For good reasons, corn snakes are considered one of the best pet snakes. They are beautiful, available in a "cornucopia" (borrowing breeders Bill and Kathy Love's colorful expression) of colors and patterns, of moderate size, and generally docile and easy to handle. Moreover, they are hardy and easy to maintain. Although they have the reputation of being secretive, with the proper vivarium design corn snakes make outstanding displays and work well with the methods presented in this book. In terms of natural morphs, the striking orange and red Okeetee morph is the best for natural displays.

Vivarium Design

Unlike those typically seen in the hobby, taller enclosures that allow for tall plants and climbing areas are better than low enclosures. Corn snakes generally fare well on a BSS substrate. Raised basking sites are key to attractive corn snake displays; create basking sites with elevated shelves or thick branch forks. After a few days of acclimation, most corn snakes will develop extended daily basking sessions on these raised shelves. Use live trees as decoration, placed in relation to climbing and resting branches to provide shade rather than climbing areas. Ficus Monique, a shrublike cultivar of weeping fig with tough leaves, works well, as do dracaenas, umbrella plants, and the *Balfour aralia*. In larger setups, include

The corn snake is without a doubt one of the most beautiful and adaptable of the snakes bred in captivity. Selective breeding has resulted in many different attractive forms.

Chamaedorea palms. Bromeliads, such as Neoregelias, can serve as shelters for babies. Like many other serpents, shedding corn snakes will hide in ground-level shelters or burrow and coil in moist substrate.

Handling

Corn snakes are among the most docile and easily handled of all snakes. For this and other reasons, they are considered one of the best pet snakes in the world.

Feeding

Baby corn snakes vary in their readiness to start feeding on pink mice because their natural diet consists of lizards and small frogs. Some require coaxing and teasing to start feeding. Larger corn snakes all readily feed on live or thawed frozen mice.

Breeding
If you cool them and put pairs together in early spring, corn snakes will breed. They are among the most easily bred of snakes and hobbyists produce thousands annually.

American Rat Snake *(Elaphe obsoleta)*
The American rat snake is a large, semiarboreal species widely distributed throughout the eastern half of the United States. The five subspecies show great variation in size, color, pattern, and temperament. They range from mostly black to gray white to brilliant solid orange. Arguably, the most beautiful of the natural forms is the Everglades rat snake *(Elaphe obsoleta rossalleni)*, with outstanding specimens that are mostly orange with a bright yellow underside. The largest member of the species is the black rat snake *(E. o. obsoleta)*, which can reach a length of just over 8 feet. The most cryptic colored are gray rat snakes *(E. obsoleta spiloides)*, which range from dark gray to a pale central Florida form known as the white oak rat snake, which boasts a gray white background with dark gray contrasting speckles and patterns and pale irises.

The black rat snake *(Elaphe obsoleta obsoleta)* is a large, semiarboreal colubrid that spends time resting in branches or shelves when kept in a vivarium with overhead spotlights.

Many beautiful designer morphs of American rat snakes have been established in recent years, including albinos, red albinos, leucistic specimens, and the unique black and white morph known as the licorice rat snake.

In general, American rat snakes are active, alert, and spunky individuals. Some bite readily and others are mostly docile and predictable. Wild Texas rat snakes *(E. obsoleta lindheimeri)* have the reputation of being one of the most consistently aggressive of the U.S. nonvenomous snakes. American rat snake babies are typically spunky, readily raising the front of the body into an S coil and prepared to strike and bite the hand that reaches for them. By the time they are adults, the great majority of these little nippers habituate to handling and become tame.

Selection

Most American rat snakes, even wild-caught ones, adapt well to captivity. However, some wild-caught adults constantly search for ways of escaping and will rub their snouts raw against the screen and corners of an enclosure. To prevent this, purchase captive-bred or -raised specimens. They will be adapted to enclosures and will usually become tame. The biting tendency of babies usually wanes by the time they become adult.

In the wild, Everglades rat snakes *(Elaphe obsoleta rossalleni)* are often found in trees and shrubs. By providing raised broad perches with overhead foliage, your rat snakes will spend more time in the open.

193

Vivarium Design

Because of their size, semiarboreal snakes generally require large caging, at least 4 feet long and 3 to 4 feet tall for adults. These snakes also prefer at least 50 percent relative humidity, so they generally fare well with a BSS substrate. American rat snakes use shelves and tree forks for resting and basking. Fig trees and dwarf umbrella plants are appropriate for baby rat snakes to climb, but for adults use these trees as backgrounds, with dry branch perches placed in front. Low-growing plants and shrubs can be included at ground level, leaving at least 50 percent open area. These snakes will use a variety of shelter types, including open-front, lateral, and raised shelters.

Handling

American rat snakes are visually alert and responsive (some people would say reactive is a better term) snakes that attract keepers that prefer snakes with spunk. Typically, babies are nippy little terrors, S coiling and raising the front of their bodies with open mouths ready to

A vivarium housing radiated rat snakes is landscaped with Ficus Monique and *Hoya carnosa variegata*.

This leucistic Texas rat snake *(Flaphe obsoleta lindheimeri)* is shown in an aggressive posture. All *Elaphe obsoleta* will bask during the day if provided with raised shelves under incandescent spotlights.

strike. In time and with regular handling, most become quite docile.

Feeding
At all ages, American rat snakes feed on rodents of the appropriate size (body thickness equal to 25 percent greater than the snake's midbody). Feed them every ten to fourteen days.

Breeding
These snakes will breed easily if cooled down and allowed to fast for two to three months during the winter.

Trans Pecos Rat Snake *(Bogertrophis subocularis)*
This beautiful U.S. species has a crisp black pattern against a rich tan background. It is mostly nocturnal and is characterized by its large eyes, the light iris contrasting sharply with the dark pupil. Its nocturnal habits make it less than ideal for a daytime display, but this species will

This is the blonde phase of the Trans Pecos rat snake *(Bogertrophis subocularis)*. It is primarily a nocturnal species and fares well in desert-type vivaria. Observe it at night under low-wattage red incandescent bulbs.

often rest on high spots (raised shelters and shelves) in view of observers. The Trans Peco rat snake is a good choice for a nocturnal display using red lights or moonlights.

Selection
Several morphs, including a blonde morph and a dramatic blue white and gray anerythristic morph, are now produced in captivity by specialists. More recently, an albino morph of this species has been established.

Vivarium Design
This terrestrial rat snake likes a large, sandy desert vivarium with a dry surface and lots of open space. Use rocks and dried wood to create shelters and basking sites, as long as they are securely anchored to prevent accidental crushing. Include large, sturdy, arid-adapted plants for decorative purposes. Provide ground-level or open-front shelters. Daytime temperatures should reach into the 80s F during the day and drop into the high 70s F at night during the warm months of the year.

Handling
This species is usually tame, although, like all rat snakes, it tends to be restless when in hand.

Feeding

Trans Pecos rat snakes of all ages will usually readily feed on mice.

Breeding

Trans Pecos rat snakes will breed readily after a period of winter cooling, but reproductive activity usually occurs later than in most colubrids, typically in the summer. Females lay up to eleven eggs in September or October. Incubation of eggs takes slightly longer than usual with most egg-laying snakes, between ten and fourteen weeks.

Asian Rat Snakes

Several species of Asian rat snake are regularly available. Increasing numbers of species are captive-bred by specialists. Several of the Asian rat snakes are semiarboreal and rank among the best display snakes. For the most part, the interest in imported Asian rat snakes is limited to specialists because of the high level of disease and parasitism, difficulty in acclimation, and mortality in wild-collected snakes.

Selection

Whenever possible, buy only captive-bred Asian rat snakes. Imports are often sick or heavily parasitized and should only be considered by those experienced in acclimating wild-collected snakes. Paying several times the price of an import for a captive-bred specimen can end up a bargain, considering the rate of mortality.

If dealing with imports, be very strict about quarantine procedures. Captive-bred individuals are hardy and typically live for many years.

Trinket Snake *(Elaphe helenae)*

At a maximum length of 5 feet, the trinket snake, a rat snake originally from India and Pakistan, is an ideal vivarium candidate. It is attractive in a subtle way, primarily because of the high-contrast pattern on the head and front part of the body. The trinket snake is semiarboreal and displays the high level of alertness expected from rat snakes.

Selection

Trinket snakes are available primarily as captive-bred babies and generally adapt well to captivity.

Vivarium Design

This species fares well in a BSS system or with potting soil as substrate. Half the surface area should be open space. Provide branches, as this species likes to climb, and include shrub-type plants in the setup.

Feeding

Trinket snakes readily feed on mice at all ages.

Handling

Like most rat snakes, the trinket snake is active and restless when in hand. Captive-raised individuals are consistently tame.

Breeding

This species is easy to breed following the standard cool-in-the-winter, introduce-snakes-in-the-spring formula. It will breed readily after a two-month cooling period in the 60s F.

The Taiwan beauty snake *(Elaphe taeniura friesii)* is a large, semiarboreal rat snake that grows up to 7 feet long. Adults require a large enclosure with raised shelves or thick, horizontal branches.

Taiwan Beauty Snake *(Elaphe taeniura friesi)*

This is a large, impressive, semiarboreal rat snake that can reach a length of 7 feet. It is also the most readily available and most commonly bred of the Asian rat snakes. It is a good selection if you're looking for a large colubrid that generally displays well.

Selection

Captive-bred Taiwan beauty snakes are regularly available from specialized breeders. Imports of this subspecies and other subspecies of beauty snake are occasionally available, but, as with all Asian rat snakes, they require experience to establish in captivity.

Handling

If captive-raised, most beauty snakes will become semi-tame but remain restless. Like American rat snakes, this species has spunk.

Vivarium Design

Keep these semiarboreal snakes in large, tall enclosures with shelves or arboreal perches, including branch forks as basking sites. A moist BSS substrate and robust small trees or shrubs help provide a comfortable setting and raise humidity.

Feeding

This species feeds readily on mice when young and on small rats when adult.

Breeding

Winter cooling into the low 60s F is sufficient for breeding this species. Females lay up to ten large eggs.

Related Species

The Blue Beauty Snake (*Elaphe taeniura*)

This is an impressive blue gray morph from Vietnam that has become very popular in recent years. Its care is generally similar to that for the Taiwan beauty snake.

Green Red-Tailed Rat Snake (*Gonyosoma oxycephalum*)

This is an impressive Asian arboreal species with populations ranging from shiny bright green to various shades of tan and gray. The tail is seldom bright red, but more typically a faded pastel red. Some populations lack a red

The stinking goddess rat snake *(Elaphe carinata)* has a subtle beauty, in part because of its intricate high-contrast pattern. In spite of its derogatory name, it is quite popular among rat snake aficionados.

tail, their tails the same color as the body. At a length of close to 7 feet (depending on the population), it is one of the largest of the green-colored colubrids and has special appeal for those seeking large snakes. The lines are very clean and the scales smooth and shiny. A striking feature is its blue and black tongue, which it exposes and wags up and down when it feels threatened or detects potential food. Most imports arrive stressed, parasitized, and diseased; a significant percentage dies in the initial stages of acclimation. Because establishing this species requires experience, it is not recommended for beginners. Once

The unusual color of this form of Vietnamese blue beauty snake (*Elaphe taeniura*) caused a sensation when it first became available in the 1990's. Its care is similar to the Taiwan beauty snake.

deparasitized and acclimated, the green red-tailed rat snake is reasonably hardy and will breed. It does not appear to have a defined breeding season and under the right conditions can breed more than once a year.

This snake likes heat, humidity, light, ventilation, and raised branches and platforms for perching. Its arboreal habits make it an ideal choice for those wanting tall, planted displays. It tends to be nippy, so take care when handling or performing vivarium maintenance. Unfortunately, this attractive species is not readily available, in part because its appeal is limited to specialists.

Vivarium Design

The minimum vivarium size for adults is a standard 48-inch-long, 55-gallon tank. An arboreal setup with BSS and trees and branches that allow coiling above the ground suits this species. Relative humidity should be 70 to 80 percent. Lightly mist nightly and keep temperatures consistently warm, in the 80s F during the day and dropping to the mid-70s F at night.

Handling

Green red-tailed rat snakes have the reputation of being biters that eventually tolerate brief handling. Specimens that are captive raised are more likely to become tame.

Diet

Green red-tailed rat snakes readily feed on appropriate sized mice at all sizes.

Breeding

Green red-tailed rat snakes are tropical and require little cooling to induce breeding. Once established, this species can breed year round and produce two to three clutches a year.

Amur Rat Snake *(Elaphe schrencki schrencki)*

This species is commonly offered under the name of Russian rat snake. It is not readily available, but hobbyists who work with them rate them among the very best of snakes. Amur rat snakes are attractive, shiny black with pale yellow bands, and a black head with yellow labial scales. They grow to a moderate, easy-to-accommodate length, with very large specimens just exceeding 5½ feet. They tend to be docile and calm and have strong arboreal tendencies, making them good display snakes. Placing spotlights over branches or raised areas will almost ensure that these snakes spend several hours daily basking in the open.

Rarely available as imports or captive-bred specimens, *Elaphe schrenki anomala*, from northeast China and western Korea, is characterized by a pale mustard brown background.

CHAPTER 22:

KINGSNAKES AND MILK SNAKES

Common Kingsnakes *(Lampropeltis getula)*

The common kingsnake is one of the most widely distributed snakes found in the United States. Moderate size, relatively calm demeanor, ease of care, and attractive patterns and color have made them among the most popular snakes in the world. Thousands are bred annually by hobbyists and commercial breeders. Most, if captive-raised, become tame.

The various subspecies show a great deal of variation, ranging from the pale, almost tweed pattern of southern Florida specimens, to the crisp striped or banded patterns of California kingsnakes. Breeders have also selectively bred outstanding morphs of kingsnakes, including albinos,

The blaze phase of the blotched kingsnake (*Lampropeltis getula goini*) comes in several attractive morphs.

hypomelanistic, and a variety of California kingsnakes. Other popular forms include the variable and very beautiful blotched kingsnakes (once recognized as a subspecies *L. getula goini*, but now reduced to a population morph from central Florida), black kingsnakes, *L. getula nigra*, and Mexican black kingsnake, *L. getula nigrita*.

Vivarium Design

Most kingsnakes fare well on a sandy soil or BSS substrate. California kingsnakes have also been maintained successfully on an all-sand substrate. The vivarium should have at least two-thirds open area, as well as shelters. Kingsnakes vary in their behaviors, depending on the subspecies and their origins. They will spend most of the day hidden in a shelter, but come out to bask in the morning and late afternoon. They use both ground-level and raised basking sites (such as flat cork bark) if not placed too high above the ground. Bushy plants and small treelike plants such as figs can be included in their displays. For desert forms like the desert-phase California kingsnakes and desert kingsnakes, arid-adapted plants are more appropriate and give the design a natural appearance.

Kingsnakes follow the typical snake pattern of being active when hungry, hiding with periods of basking after a meal, and hiding or partially burrowing in substrate when in shed.

The banana phase California kingsnake was produced through selective breeding by herpetoculturists.

Feeding

Common kingsnakes in the wild are indiscriminate feeders, consuming a wide range of reptilian (including other snakes and occasionally baby turtles) and mammalian prey. In captivity, almost all will readily feed on mice of the appropriate size. Once adult, their gluttonous habits make them prone to obesity, so limit the amount of food offered per feeding.

Shown is the tangerine phase of the Honduran milk snake *(Lampropeltis triangulum hondurensis)*. If kept in a dimly lit cage, this large milk snake will occasionally come out during the day. It ranks as one of the finest tricolors for display because of its size (up to 5 feet) and vivid coloration.

Breeding

These are colubrid formula breeders. Cool them during the winter and introduce pairs together in the spring and they will breed. There is a great interest in establishing and developing new designer morphs through selective breeding.

Tricolor Milk Snakes and Kingsnakes

These colorful banded members of the genus *Lampropeltis* used to be among the most popular snake species in the hobby, until it became apparent that their behaviors in LAM setups made them dull fare. They are generally highly

The Pueblan milk snake *(Lampropeltis triangulum campbelli)* is one of the most readily available of the milk snakes. It tends to be secretive and nocturnal.

interesting to snake hobbyists, but less appealing to the pet-seeking public. Most are secretive, crepuscular or nocturnal, and nervous when handled. The challenge, and it is one that should be tackled by commercial breeders, is to develop vivarium designs that make the keeping of these beautiful snakes more enjoyable.

Selection

Research carefully before you buy a tricolor milk snake or kingsnake because the different species and subspecies vary significantly in size, requirements, and habits. Their habitats range from desert scrub to woodlands and tropical forest. Most species are now available only as captive-bred animals and generally do well in captivity.

Vivarium Design

The obvious challenge with tricolor kingsnakes and milk snakes in general is in dealing with secretive or nocturnal species that, given a choice, will spend most of their time invisible and inside a shelter. To enjoy keeping these species requires ingenuity in the vivarium design and pushing limits in terms of shaping behavior.

Depending on a species and its requirements, several factors must be considered to make it a better display. As a general rule, tricolor snakes are crepuscular or nocturnal and will avoid being in the open in bright light. Overhead shelters that provide large areas of shade can increase the chances of some species emerging during the day. For example, forest species, such as Honduran and Andean milk snakes, can be displayed with an open-front shelter, a BSS forest substrate, and plants to provide shade. Under those conditions they will come out frequently and may even bask in an area that corresponds to a forest edge, where heat and light are available at the outskirts of shadows.

In general, if the lighting is not too bright and the background temperature is not too high, several species will come out and spend periods of time in the open on a basking site. To prevent exposure to bright light, the basking site should be heated with a ceramic infrared heating unit instead of a bright incandescent bulb.

Another method to better display tricolors is to eliminate closed shelters and use only raised open-front shelters that allow for viewing during the day. Some hobbyists anchor flat rocks to the background with spaces between them so they can serve as shelters. The snakes are visible coiled between rocks at the back of the vivarium.

When using open-front shelters in tanks with screen tops, increase the relative humidity when these snakes are in shed. One of the functions of shelters in the wild is to reduce evaporative water loss by providing a zone with a higher relative humidity than the open air. In vivaria, most snakes will easily replenish lost water by drinking, but too low a relative humidity can dry out their skin and cause shedding problems. To prevent this, place a plastic storage box with a moist cypress mulch or sphagnum moss in the enclosure when you notice the snake is in shed.

Another method for displaying tricolor kingsnakes and milk snakes is to construct underground shelters with a front viewing window. Also, red lights allow for viewing of these species at night.

Feeding

Most adult tricolor *Lampropeltis* spp. readily feed on mice of the appropriate size, although smaller forms may have a preference for lizards and will need to be trained to take mice. Most babies of the larger species will readily feed on mice, but babies of smaller species generally have a preference for lizards and, assuming they are even large enough, it requires considerable effort to convince them to take a pinkie mouse. Scenting mice with skink tails or other lizards is one method to convince baby tricolor kingsnakes to eat mice.

Handling
None of the tricolor kingsnakes or milk snakes are great handling snakes. They tend to be restless and writhe. The most calm and probably the best choice for a pet tricolor is the Mexican milk snake *(Lampropeltis triangulum annulata)*. Other species, such as Andean milk snakes and Honduran milk snakes, although restless when young, become amenable to handling as adults.

Andean Milk Snake *(Lampropeltis triangulum andesiana)*: This large, impressive species can reach a length of 4½ feet. It can be kept on a forest BSS substrate. The Andean milk snake likes cooler temperatures, in the low to mid-70s F during the day with a basking site of 80° F.

Honduran Milk Snake *(Lampropeltis triangulum hondurensis)*: This large species can grow to 4 feet. Its size and the availability of spectacular captive-bred morphs make it one of the more impressive display snakes. It can be kept in a forest-type vivarium with plants and short trees that generate shade. Provide at least 50 percent open area. With regular handling, this species can become relatively docile.

Mexican Milk Snake *(Lampropeltis triangulum annulata)*: This moderate-sized snake reaches 2½ feet and adapts well to captivity. It is the most amenable to handling of the tricolors. If not kept too warm, this species will come out in the open during the day to bask. It is best kept in a desert or dry-surface, woodland-type vivarium.

Gray-Banded Kingsnake *(Lampropeltis alterna)*: This is one of the most beautiful U.S. snakes. Several forms, divided into the alterna (gray with black bands) and Blair phases (gray and black and orange bands), are now bred in some numbers by specialists. Gray-banded kingsnakes are nocturnal desert snakes that fare well in vivaria with a rock landscape, at least 50 percent open area, and few plants. Open-front shelters help make them more visible. Babies are lizard specialists and commonly require lizards or lizard-scented pink mice to start feeding. Adults are typically 3 to 4 feet in length. The gray-banded kingsnake requires winter cooling into the 50s for successful breeding.

Breeding
Most tricolor kingsnakes and milk snakes are colubrid formula breeders. Cool them in the winter, put the sexes together in early spring, and they will breed.

The Gray-banded kingsnake *(Lampropeltis alterna)* is a gorgeous U.S. desert species regularly bred by specialists. Display them in vivaria with open-front rock shelters. At night, observe them under low-wattage red incandescent lights.

CHAPTER 23:
OTHER SNAKES

Rough Green Snakes *(Opheodrys aestivus)*

During late spring and summer, these pretty, slender, green U.S. snakes are offered by the thousands in the pet trade. Unfortunately, because they are considered cheap, disposable children's pets, most die from neglect and over-handling within a few months of captivity. This is a great shame, because the rough green snake is an outstanding vivarium candidate. It fares well in planted vivaria and, because of its insectivorous diet, can be kept in mixed-species tanks with small lizards and medium-sized tree frogs.

Vivarium Design

The rough green snake fares best in naturalistic vivaria because it enjoys plants for climbing and plants help maintain the relative humidity. It also fares well using the BSS method. Provide a large water container, as well as some dry wood and live shrubby plants. Ground-level shelters can also be used. The last specimens I kept were maintained in a

The rough green snake *(Opheodrys aestivus)* is a small, diurnal, insect-eating U.S. species that fares best in naturalistic vivaria with plants and climbing areas.

tank with skunk geckos *(Gecko vittatus)* for over a year, after which the setup was donated to a school.

This diurnal snake requires light and may benefit from a full-spectrum bulb, although a full-spectrum bulb is not required if the diet is properly supplemented.

Feeding
These snakes readily feed on crickets of the appropriate size. Lightly dust crickets with the calcium/vitamin mineral powder used for insectivorous lizards. Offer rough green snakes as much food as they will eat two to three times a week.

Water
In addition to a sizeable water bowl, mist once daily.

Health Problems
Rough green snakes are often maintained under crowded, unhygienic conditions for days or weeks prior to entering the pet trade. As a result, some may be infected with parasites. Mite infections are common in store-purchased rough green snakes and are quickly fatal if untreated, in part because rough green snakes (compared to most snakes) have a high skin-surface to volume ratio. Large numbers of mites colonizing the large skin area can quickly cause anemia from loss of blood.

Breeding
If kept in groups of one or more pairs, rough green snakes will breed after a period of winter cooling and reduced

photoperiod. The babies are tiny but can be raised on crickets of the appropriate size. Babies primarily drink from droplets formed by misting.

Black Racer *(Coluber constrictor)*

Racer is a common name for several species of medium to large non-constricting colubrids (don't get fooled by the scientific name) that have the reputation of being fast, nippy, nervous, wary, active, and difficult to acclimate to captivity. The most readily available is the common black racer *(Coluber constrictor constrictor)* and its many sub-species. The most attractive form is the white-blotched subspecies known as the buttermilk racer *(C. constrictor anthicus)* found in Louisiana, eastern Texas, and southern Arkansas. From a display point of view, racers have several desirable features; they are mostly diurnal, semiarboreal, active, and alert. I rank these sleek alert snakes among the more interesting snakes to keep and display, even if they are not the most beautiful.

Selection

Whenever possible, start with small specimens that are around 24 inches in length. Wild-caught adults are nervous and easily stressed and require special conditions for acclimation. This species is usually not captive bred.

Vivarium

Racers do best kept singly in relatively large enclosures, long enough for the snakes to comfortably and completely extend their bodies. At least two-thirds of their vivarium should be open area, with large sections of dried wood and small shrubs or trees for basking and perching. Provide a ground-level shelter and a large, shallow water container.

Feeding

Medium to adult specimens readily feed on mice. Babies may have to be fed tree frogs or lizard-scented mice initially. You can also feed cut sections of prekilled mice, such as the base of tails or limb sections.

Handling

This species is nervous when handled and moves quickly. Wild-caught adults readily bite. If raised from babies, racers can be docile, although they are not likely to remain still when in hand.

Breeding

Black racers are not bred by hobbyists, but presumably this egg-laying species could be bred using the standard colubrid formula.

Egyptian diadem snakes *(Spalerosophis diadema cliffordi)* may not have bright colors but in terms of activity and behaviors, they're an entertaining display snake ideal for desert vivaria. Unlike most snakes, this species is usually active during the day.

Diadem Snakes (*Spalerosophis* spp.)

Diadem snakes are often only appreciated by those who take the time to recognize their special qualities. They tend to be restless when handled and some, like the royal diadem snake, may also hiss and occasionally strike and bite. The great qualities of diadem snakes are their attractive appearance, high level of alertness, and propensity for diurnal activity. They make very entertaining display snakes.

Selection

The most commonly available diadem snake is the faded tan and brown blotched Egyptian diadem snake *(Spalerosophis d. cliffordi)*, which is imported sporadically. More rarely, you can find imported Pakistan *(S. arenarius)* and royal diadem snakes *(S. atriceps)*. The latter are also bred in small numbers by specialized hobbyists. Compared to most imported serpents, diadem snakes often arrive in

It is impossible to predict the adult coloring of this hatchling black-headed diadem snake as the species undergoes a dramatic shift in color and pattern as it matures.

relatively good health, although I recommend treating them for internal parasites, notably nematodes. When available, captive-specimens are always preferable.

Vivarium Design

All diadem snakes fare well in planted desert vivaria with large open spaces. Use sand or a sandy BSS mix as a substrate. Include bush-type plants, broad wood sections, and angled cork bark, as these species will often climb on ground structures. They also commonly bask on raised areas, such as stacked rock, wood, or shelves. The standard desert plant fare, such as pony-tailed palms, snake plants, haworthia, elephant bush, and caudexed figs, work well with these snakes. Diadem snakes like it hot during the day and should be provided with basking sites that reach 85–90° F. At night the temperature can drop into the 70s F.

Feeding

Diadem snakes feed primarily on lizards when young, but are easily switched to mice. They are active hunters that have a preference for live, moving prey or freshly killed prey jiggled on forceps. All diadem snakes commonly go through periods of fasting, lasting several months during the winter and intermittently for several weeks during the course of the year. These snakes drink little and may obtain much of their water from metabolic breakdown of food.

Breeding

Diadem snakes have been bred following a standard colubrid-breeding regimen with a winter cooling period in the 50s to low 60s F.

Wart Snakes (*Acrochordus* spp.)

Once available with some regularity, these odd aquatic snakes have become rare both in the hobby and in zoo collections. Because they have specialized requirements and a low reproductive rate, they are only recommended for experienced and dedicated hobbyists. Of the species available, the black and white wart snake *(Acrochordus granulatus)*, once imported in small numbers from the Philippines, is the best pet snake. It is by far the most beautiful and, because of its small size, the most suitable for keeping indoors. If they can be established, black and white wart snakes rank among the top display snakes in the world. Because of their rarity and low reproductive rate, hobbyists should make every effort to develop methods to successfully keep and breed these snakes in captivity. As it stands, they are seldom available and it may not be long before they are not available at all.

Selection

Avoid specimens with multiple skin sores. If only a few sores are present, keeping them in the proper conditions

The elephant trunk snake *(Acrochordus javanicus)* is seldom kept in captivity, but their good display potential and unusual habits warrant further work to establish them in captivity.

described below may allow them to fight off infection and survive. Prompt treatment with antibiotics and provision of high-quality warm water must be implemented immediately if a skin infection shows signs of spreading.

Handling

Wart snakes should never be handled. They are built to survive in the reduced gravity of water.

Vivarium Design

Wart snakes are interesting because they are aquatic and spend all their time almost completely submerged. They can be displayed and kept in aquaria, like fish. Two of the three species live in brackish water, so adding salt (one teaspoon of rock salt per gallon) to the water may help reduce the risk of skin infections. The largest species, the elephant trunk snake *(Acrochordus javanicus)*, can be kept in fresh water.

Most captive specimens end up dying of skin infections that eventually become systemic. The cause is usually related to water quality. These snakes require high-quality water, like fish, and a great deal of attention needs to be given to providing effective filtration to maintain the low ammonia and nitrite levels required to keep them healthy. Providing biologically active silt as a substrate may serve as a probiotic preventative of skin infections. These aquatic snakes do not thermoregulate through basking because they live exclusively in water. Maintain water temperature around 80° F year round through the use of a submersible water heater. They give birth to live young.

CHAPTER 24:

THE FUTURE

Where Do We Go From Here?

I am convinced that the art of keeping snakes is the next stage of development in the snake-keeping hobby. It raises the hobby to the level of an art form and consequently puts the keeping of snakes in captivity in a new perspective, with many economic and cultural implications. The following are some of the changes possible in a future where the art of keeping snakes becomes more popular and widespread.

Display Marketing

The captive-bred snake market has experienced modest declines, even plateaued, in the last five years. One reason is that there was a saturation of the snake-investment market; as a result, many commercial and hobbyist breeders dropped out of the business. The problem with breeding snakes as an investment is that their value's longevity is determined by their generation time and reproductive rates. Given half a chance, many snakes are reliable breeding machines. What starts off as a rarity and good investment prospect can become relatively low-priced standard fare in the pet trade by the fourth or fifth generation. On the bright side, increasing numbers of people are choosing to own snakes not as a breeding investment but for their display potential and the enjoyment they provide as a form of living art.

Unfortunately, most commercial breeders remain stuck in the marketing of snakes as investments, emphasizing snake-keeping under LAM conditions and failing to realize the market potential of methods that emphasize aesthetic display. The obvious beauty of most snakes can be either highlighted or subdued by the context of its presentation.

Too often the LAM setups in which breeders market their snakes are the stuff of basements and closed rooms, not suitable for viewing by visitors. If someone breeds outstanding gray-banded kingsnakes or Asian rat snakes, I'd like them to show me how I can display them in ways that will add to the beauty of my home and that will be a source of viewing pleasure. Don't just sell me the snake. Show me the whole picture, give me a vision of the possibilities. I hope the future will bring a new era in snake marketing by the commercial breeders that have made this wonderful hobby possible.

Systems Herpetoculture: The Ultimate Challenge

Systems herpetoculture is considered the most advanced and sophisticated branch of herpetoculture, practiced by a very small number of hobbyists and a few specialists in designing complex public displays. It is an experimental method for designing vivarium displays that combine a variety of plants and animals into a type of contained ecosystem. There are no set rules unless you are concerned with a biotope approach—attempting to match species from similar areas, countries, or continents.

Each successful design becomes a specific formula for combining plant and animal species, resulting in a type of herpetocultural ecosystem. The results are different than a natural ecosystem; first, because the combinations are artificial and, second, because several of the components of the system are provided by the hobbyist, such as food and water. Systems herpetoculture is only possible in relatively large enclosures with a perimeter at least twice the total length of the snake(s) being maintained.

Within the space limitations of most vivaria, the application of systems herpetoculture is limited to certain snake species. Gluttonous, relatively indiscriminate feeders, such as milk snakes and kingsnakes, are difficult if not impossible choices for systems herpetoculture, while more specialized feeders allow a diversity of nonprey animals to be included.

In systems herpetoculture, start with a bioactive substrate system, then add the landscape elements and plants recommended for the primary species—the snake or snakes you intend to keep. Then, add landscape structures that will not interfere with the needs of the primary species to create niches for secondary species. For example, you might add bromeliads that will not interfere with the welfare of an arboreal snake but will provide a niche that allows the inclusion of a certain frog. Or you might add vertical sections of bark that can be used by certain lizards. The design and selection requires a careful evaluation of the needs and possible interrelationships of different species. For obvious reasons, secondary species— if they are to survive—should have generally similar environmental requirements as the primary species, but must fall outside of the prey selection range of that species.

I have one setup that was built with an aquarium. I placed a fiberglass rock background and added a 2-inch layer of decomposed granite sand as a substrate bottom. In the middle ground, I put sections of driftwood on which I anchored (using monofilament line, which is available at hardware stores) Java moss and Java fern plantlets. In the substrate I planted *Bacopa carolinensis, Sagittaria subulata*, vallisnerias, and various cryptocorynes. I wedged a large section of cork bark between two sides of the tank and added water to three-quarters the height of the tank, allowing cork bark and driftwood sections to rise above the water line. A small external power filter filters the water and two fluorescent bulbs running the length of the tank light the setup. A small incandescent fixture rests above the cork bark to provide a basking site. For fish, I included white clouds, gold barbs, and American flagfish. I added a captive-hatched baby razor back musk turtle and a baby banded water snake. Two years later, almost everyone has grown and fared well except for some of the fish, which were replaced as they disappeared. The overly curious and less wary fish fell prey to the turtle or the water snake. Those that survived have learned to avoid these species. The white clouds have bred in the setup and some of the babies have grown to adulthood. One of the secrets to this kind of setup is providing a large, deep-water area, allowing sanctuary for the fish to escape predation.

Rough green snakes are generally good candidates for the systems herpetoculture because they are insectivorous and harmless to medium-sized geckos, anoles, and tree frogs. In large shoreline vivaria, it is even possible to combine fish, anoles, geckos, frogs, and rough green snakes. Various invertebrates can be added, including ramshorn snails in the water and medium to large millipedes on land.

I have also successfully combined tree frogs, poison frogs, small lizards, and giant millipedes in tropical forest vivaria housing medium boa constrictors or emerald tree boas. Because of the creative and theoretical challenges it provides, systems herpetoculture may be the most exciting area of herpetoculture today.

Snake Vivaria as Educational Tools

Few tools are more exciting for teaching biology and ecology than vivaria. Well-designed vivaria using the methods presented in *The Art of Keeping Snakes* provide the means for integrating certain aspects of nature in culture and offer unique opportunities for learning about the natural world. Systems herpetoculture is one of the most valuable of all educational tools for teaching biology and the basic concepts of ecology. As a guide, I have listed some of the topics that could be studied from observation, testing, and measurement of the materials and organisms potentially contained in snake vivaria:

- Soil science, soil chemistry, and bioactivity of soil systems
- Waste recycling in nature
- Biology and function of bacteria, fungi, protozoa, algae, and a variety of invertebrates
- Plants: the kinds of plants, their biology and their role in ecology
- Thermal dynamics in nature
- Sunlight: the light spectrum and its qualities and functions

- Reptiles and snakes: their biological characteristics, evolution, and behaviors
- The characteristics of snakes and how they are used to determine their taxonomy and systematics
- Food composition, ingestion, and its relationship to growth rate
- Biology and behaviors of secondary species used in the display
- Geography as it applies to captive species
- Water: pH, hardness, ammonia, nitrites, and nitrates
- Food chains: Plants to bacteria to invertebrates to vertebrate prey to snake
- The physics of movement and related physiology, such as energy expenditure

Conclusion

In the process of researching and developing the methods for the *Art of Keeping Snakes*, my personal interest in snakes was rekindled and my outlook on the hobby changed. Several species I once considered the least interesting and challenging to keep have turned out to be among my favorite snakes to observe and enjoy. Applying the art of keeping snakes gave me the opportunity to notice evidence of learning and adaptation in snakes I had previously missed, for obvious reasons. It turns out that, like people, snakes that are not challenged or stimulated only express a limited range of behaviors. When maintained under LAM conditions, such as the plastic trays and boxes favored by many breeders or the bare-bones setups promoted by most pet stores, snakes can seem downright dull. On the other hand, when introduced to a well-designed naturalistic vivarium, many snakes seem to slowly come alive again. They investigate their environment, develop adaptive patterns of behavior, and settle in.

As a result of experimenting with the methods presented here, my reasons for keeping snakes have also changed. I used to consider captive breeding the primary reason for keeping snakes, now I derive more enjoyment from keeping single specimens or pairs in vivaria and observing their behaviors. Whether they breed or not has become secondary. The focus of my involvement in the hobby has shifted. It is no longer just keeping a species alive, but assembling a composition, a type of system, with an emphasis on aesthetics and an impression on the mind, like a work of art. I no longer invite friends to see my kingsnake, but rather my kingsnake display. I notice that guests now react to both the snake and the idea of encapsulated nature as art.

These experiments and the reactions they elicited were the reasons I wrote this book. The result is a rough map into what I believe is a new area of ideas that will set the course for the future of our hobby. I invite readers to explore this new territory and find out for themselves what I am trying to convey—that the vivarium in your living room can be a doorway.

RESOURCES

Barker D. and T. Barker. 1994. *Pythons of the World*. Volume I. Australia. Advanced Vivarium Systems: Irvine, CA.

Chiras, S. 2000. "Care and Breeding of Australia's Diamond Pythons," *Reptiles*. 8 (4):44-57.

Conway, J. 1999. "Solomon Islands Ground Boas: Captive Care and Propagation," *The Vivarium*. 10(6):30-31.

Conway, J. 1998. "Island Gems: The Pacific Boas (Candoia)," *Reptiles*. 6 (10):48-59.

De Vosjoli, P. 1998. *The Boa Constrictor Manual*. Irvine, CA: Advanced Vivarium Systems.

De Vosjoli, P., Barker D., Barker T., and R. Klingenberg. 1995. *The Ball Python Manual*. Irvine, CA: Advanced Vivarium Systems.

De Vosjoli, P., Donoghue, S., and R. Klingenberg. 1999. "The Multifactorial Model of Herpetoculture. Part 1: Ontogeny." *The Vivarium*. 11 (1)

Kluge A.G. 1991. *Boine Snake Phylogeny and Research Cycles*. Misc. Pub. Mus. of Zool. University of Michigan No. 178.

Love, B. and K. Love. 1999. *The Corn Snake Manual*. Irvine, CA: Advanced Vivarium Systems.

Perlowin, D. 1994. *The General Care and Maintenance of Garter Snakes and Water Snakes*. Irvine, CA: Advanced Vivarium Systems.

Perlowin, D. 1992. *General Care and Breeding of Common Kingsnakes*. Irvine, CA: Advanced Vivarium Systems.

Stafford P.J. and R.W. Henderson. 1996. *Kaleidoscopic Tree Boas. The Genus Corallus of Tropical America*. Malabar, FL: Krieger Publishing Company.

Rossi, J. 1992. *Snakes of the Eastern United States and Canada: Keeping Them Healthy in Captivity*. Malabar, FL: Krieger Publishing Company.

Trutnau, Ludwig. 1986. *Nonvenomous Snakes. A Comprehensive Guide to Care and Breeding of over 100 species*. New York: Barron's Educational Series, Inc.

INDEX

ABOUT THE AUTHOR

Philippe de Vosjoli is a highly acclaimed author of best-selling reptile-care books. His work in the field of herpetoculture has been recognized nationally and internationally for establishing high standards for amphibian and reptile care. His books, articles, and other writings have been praised and recommended by numerous herpetological societies, veterinarians, and other experts in the field. Philippe de Vosjoli was also the cofounder and president of The American Federation of Herpetoculturists, and was given the Josef Laszlo Memorial Award in 1995 for excellence in herpetoculture and his contribution to the advancement of the field.